LIVING
Untangled

Healing From Abuse and Discovering the Heart of God

by Michelle Perez

Scripture taken from the New King James Version®. Copyright © 1982 by Thomas Nelson. Used by permission. All rights reserved.

National Domestic Violence Hotline. (n.d.). *What is domestic violence?* The National Domestic Violence Hotline. https://www.thehotline.org/resources/what-is-domestic-violence/

Disclaimers

Legal & Privacy Notice
This memoir represents my personal memories and opinions. Events are described as I recall them; dialogue is paraphrased. Names, roles, and timelines have been modified to protect privacy. Any resemblance to real persons is coincidental. No statement is intended as fact about any identifiable person.

Pastoral / Wellness Disclaimer
This book shares personal, faith-based reflections. It is not legal, medical, or mental-health advice. Readers should consult qualified professionals for individual guidance.

Composites Note
Some individuals and events are composites or have been modified to preserve anonymity.

Dedication

To my children, **Julia and Brian**, you had the courage to grow past the hurts handed to you. Seeing you now as extraordinary adults warms my heart. Your lives are living proof that God redeems what was broken. I love you both beyond measure, to the moon and back.

And to my husband, **Zeke**, your love, patience, and faith have been a constant reflection of God's grace. Thank you for walking beside me through this healing journey, and for believing in the purpose God placed in this story.

Table of Contents

Introduction

This book is not a timeline. It's a tapestry.

Each chapter weaves together threads of truth, pain, faith, hope, and practical support, sometimes delicate, sometimes frayed, but always woven with purpose. In *Living Untangled* the stories told in this book are stories that illustrate the topics of the chapters. It is not a chronological step-by-step retelling of one person's story, but a journey through themes that touch the survivor's heart: identity, fear, faith, and freedom. This book was written out of a desire to help women untangle the mess of the hidden wounds that abuse leaves behind and to remind every survivor that God's healing is not out of reach.

The journey toward wholeness rarely happens in a straight line; it twists through doubt, grief, and grace. Yet, even in the most tangled seasons, God's love remains constant. The reflections and stories shared here are meant to create connections and understanding. They are not meant to prescribe a single path to healing, but to affirm that there *is* a path, one guided by the God who restores what's been broken and renews what's been lost.

If you are reading this as someone who has lived through abuse, I am praying for you. I pray that these pages help you reclaim your voice and rediscover hope. If you are reading as a supporter or advocate, I pray that through reading this book you gain insight into the nature of abuse and glean information to equip you to walk gently beside those who are rebuilding their lives.

Each chapter can be read in order or revisited as needed. Let the words meet you where you are. Healing doesn't happen all at once, but it always begins with truth, compassion, and the belief that freedom is possible through Christ.

Chapter 1: Breaking the Silence

I sat on my towel, toes buried in the sand, the sun warm on my back. I stared blankly at the ocean stretching wide in front of me. My husband sat in the sand not far away. My kids played at the edge of the water, running and jumping as they happily splashed each other. Their laughter floated on the sound of the surf. To any bystander, this scene looked like we were the perfect little family.

But behind this seemingly idyllic scene lingered the trauma of what had happened only days earlier.

****

This book is not about abuse. It's about hope, the kind that grows quietly in impossible places. It's about faith that outlasts fear, and the steady hand of God that leads us out of silence and into freedom. My story is just one of many, but I share it because silence keeps too many of us bound.

While I write from the perspective of a woman, I know that men also experience abuse, and their pain is just as real and deserving of healing. But I can only speak from where I've stood, through the lens of a woman who lost her voice and slowly found it again. My prayer is that no matter who you are, the truths in these pages remind you that freedom and redemption are possible.

I also want to recognize that while I have experienced physical abuse, many others have endured wounds that can't be seen. Physical abuse is only one of the many forms of abuse. Abuse is not always marked by bruises. It can take the form of words that wound, control that confines, or manipulation that steals a person's sense of worth. All forms of abuse are dangerous, and each leaves a lasting impact on the heart and mind.

It's easy to fall into comparing stories, thinking one kind of pain is worse than another. But comparison only keeps us silent and minimizes our own truth. Every story matters, and every experience of harm deserves to be acknowledged and healed. God sees it all, the visible and the hidden, and His compassion reaches into every kind of suffering.

For years, I stayed quiet. Silence became the key to my survival. Speaking the truth out loud felt dangerous, even long after I was free, and sometimes even now. But healing began for me the moment I realized silence protects the wrong person. This story is my way of breaking that silence, one truth, one memory, one act of courage at a time.

I know how easy it was to hide behind picture-perfect moments. They made the truth harder to name. Those seemingly idyllic moments were the camouflage of our life.

****

I still remember it so clearly. Just a few short days before we left on our beach vacation, the atmosphere between my husband and I drastically shifted. The shift was sudden and jarring; the catalyst was a seemingly minor thing; he had forgotten a password to a website I had never had access to. Yet somehow, he wanted me to provide the password to him. I sat down in the desk chair. I could see the frustration on his face. Before I could even try to help him, I saw the message on the screen that an incorrect password had been used too many times. The site was locked. I remember saying something about the site being locked, and then the rest is a blur.

One moment, I was sitting in the desk chair; the next, my world had turned upside down. I was on the floor, and the chair was on its back.

I felt the crushing weight on top of me. I was pinned down, entirely powerless, trapped. I could hear his voice above me, but the words were lost in the panicked thoughts running through my mind. I struggled desperately to breathe, the terrifying reality of suffocation setting in. I remember that singular, chilling thought: this was the end of the road for me. I believed, in that moment, that I had drawn my last breath.

My mind flew to my children. My daughter was away at camp, but my son was upstairs, playing in his room. The immediate, urgent terror was not just for myself, but the thought that he might be the one to find me, or worse, that once I was silenced, he might be in danger. How could I protect him?

It felt like an eternity under that overwhelming pressure. This terrifying feeling of being physically overpowered was not entirely new, but this time my mindset shifted. This time, I refused to let fear be my final emotion. I gathered every ounce of strength I had left and forced my face into a blank, unfeeling stare. I can still see in my mind how he visibly pulled his head back and stared back at me, at first with what looked like anger, then with a look of questioning. He kept staring at me, seemingly realizing my blank expression wasn't changing; his face slowly took on the expression of newfound fear. I felt like my blank stare was something he didn't know how to respond to. I had always shown fear in these moments before. This blank stare seemed to rattle him, shaking him out of whatever headspace he was in. The pressure on my throat suddenly released. But the weight pressing into me remained; the feeling of being trapped only intensified by the sharp pressure against my arms, pinning me down.

Then came the words that shattered the fog I'd been living in. I remember him in essence, telling me that I was incapable of knowing when to leave the marriage.

I remember being called a lot of different things over the course of the marriage. But this one stunned me. Until that moment, it had never crossed my mind that the cruelty I experienced might be deliberate, that he might actually want to drive me out of the marriage. That thought hit me like a thunderclap, shattering the fog I had been living in. I froze, not knowing what to think or how to respond. And then, almost without realizing it, my response slipped out of my mouth:

"You're right."

But here I was, about a week later, sitting at the beach on what I had quietly promised myself would be our last family vacation. But now I was regretting that decision. I sat there, terrified of what might come next and praying to make it home safely. I was still trying to keep up the appearance of a perfect life. I knew I needed to pretend that everything was fine to keep my husband calm, his anger at bay, and maintain the image of a happy little family.

That moment in the office was the turning point for me. Those words telling me that I didn't know when to leave the marriage awakened me to what I had previously closed my eyes to. I now believed that staying with him would cost me my life someday soon. I knew I needed to plan a safe exit for my children and me.

I wholeheartedly believed that if I stayed quiet, I would die. My children would be left motherless. I wondered: *Would he get away with it? Would he hurt my children? Would they survive him?* These questions kept running through my mind.

The longer I stayed quiet, the more I realized I was covering the behavior that was silencing me. I couldn't do it anymore. The time had come for me to tell someone. It was time to break my silence. Time to take the first step in giving my kids the safe future they deserved. But we were in the middle of our vacation. I couldn't call the people I trusted most because every waking moment was spent close to him. The only choice I had was to text someone. But who could I text that wouldn't immediately call me? Who could I text that wouldn't want answers right this minute?

As I mentally went down the list of the people I could trust with my secret, I finally decided to text one of my sisters. We had a good relationship, but we were never "besties" in the way I was with other sisters. We talked occasionally and loved each other a lot, and I knew she would accept the words in the text and not ask for answers right then.

My hands trembled as I stared at my phone, reading and re-reading the message I was about to send my sister. I knew that once I pressed "send," there would be no turning back. Once I told her about the abuse, my coverup would no longer be an option. I would have to make a change. I would have to leave him. It was time to break my silence. My message went something like this:

I'm sending you this message because I need to hold myself accountable. I've been abused for my whole marriage, and I'm finally going to leave him. Please don't ask me questions right now, and please PLEASE don't call me. We're on vacation with the kids, and I'm terrified of what he'll do if he finds out I told anyone. I know this is pretty vague, but I'll call you once I'm home.

I knew this would shock her, but I knew she would honor my request and not call me. For years, I had kept what was happening hidden. I had mastered the art of smiling in public, bowing my head in private, and carrying the crushing weight of these secrets alone. Speaking out was shattering the perfect image I had worked so hard to project. For years I felt like I was running a full-time public relations campaign for my marriage. I carefully managed appearances, covered up the cracks, and made sure no one saw the truth. But after nearly 20 years I had come to the realization that staying silent was the slowest kind of death. It was both literally and figuratively taking the air out of my lungs. That was the prison of abuse: trapped by what is being done, haunted by what might come next, and paralyzed by the fear of saying it out loud.

For years, I rehearsed bravery in my mind. I gave myself countless pep talks, urging myself to tell someone, anyone, what was happening behind closed doors. I ached for the reassurance that leaving would be okay, that I could make it on my own. But no matter how often I tried to talk myself into having courage, the shame spoke louder. My private pep talks weren't enough to break through the fear.

Everything changed the moment I spoke up. The simple act of sending a text to my sister was the first tiny turning point in my mindset. That one decision planted a seed of confidence that no internal dialogue ever could. Action, not silent resolve, was what shifted my thoughts and helped me realize I could stand up for myself and my children.

That message to my sister may have seemed small, but it was the first sliver of courage I'd been able to muster in many years. Just a few sentences typed with trembling hands, but it was the heaviest thing I had ever sent. Abuse doesn't just bruise the body; it buries the soul under layers of embarrassment and shame. Shame is what keeps so many people silent. It whispers: *"You allowed this to happen. It's your fault. No one will ever believe you."*

For years, I believed those lies. I thought if I stayed quiet, I could protect the image of my husband and my perfect family. I thought I could protect myself, most importantly, protect my children. But silence doesn't protect anyone; it isolates and enables. Shame grows stronger when it's kept in the dark; it thrives in secrecy. But even the smallest act of courage can begin the healing process.

Speaking up felt impossible because it meant I had to strip away the mask I wore so well. It meant people would know the truth: my marriage was in shambles, I wasn't as strong and put together as I looked, and that the person I vowed to share my life with was the one causing me harm. Shame told me that if anyone found out they wouldn't believe me. I feared that if they knew, they would judge me, blame me, or turn their backs.

My life was a perfectly curated picture. To onlookers, I was the smiling wife who packed lunches, cooked dinners, and provided his perfectly starched shirts. I kept a spotless house and raised two beautiful children, all of which rounded out the picture of perfection. I was an active member of my church, leading children's divisions and women's ministries. I was the ultimate professional at work, never letting anyone see that my home life was tearing me apart. This was all part of the mask; the image I meticulously crafted to hide the chaos and violence that existed behind closed doors.

It all started shortly after we got married. It was a shock at first. I didn't want to put a label on what was happening, and I refused to label myself as a victim of abuse. I told myself I could leave if I wanted to. I chose to stay because I thought he just needed me to love and support him through this dark time in his life. I couldn't believe that this man, the one I thought would love me forever, could hurt me in this way. My mind couldn't reconcile the charming, funny person he was in public with the rage I experienced behind closed doors. My heart was broken but my mind kept saying the problem had to be me.

It wasn't long after we were married that I started an internal dialogue, making excuses for how he treated me. I told myself he must be overwhelmed with work or weighed down by the new responsibilities of married life. I told myself his outbursts were things he couldn't control. How could it ever be possible that he would *choose* to hurt me? In response, I pushed myself harder, striving to be the 'perfect' wife who could ease his stress and make him feel loved.

I prayed that God would touch my husband's heart and soften it toward me. I prayed that I could understand my husband's needs. I prayed that God would change my heart. I prayed that God would give my husband peace. It took me many years to understand that prayer isn't a magic wand that takes away someone else's free will. I finally came to realize that he had a choice and unless or until he had a personal conversion, there was nothing I could do to change his heart.

It took me way too long to recognize the truth: abuse isn't a mindless reaction that can't be controlled. I began to notice that when we were around others, he seemed calm, but when we were alone, the atmosphere changed and things often felt tense. I was afraid of what might happen next. I constantly walked on eggshells, trying desperately to keep him happy, only to face physical and emotional consequences whenever I fell short of his impossible expectations.

I grew up in a Christian home, and I was raised to believe that the only Biblical grounds for divorce was infidelity. He believed that, too. This belief shaped how we approached marriage. I viewed my marriage as if it was an alabaster egg that needed to be treated with care. Looking back, I realize that belief was the reason why I justified, minimized, and tolerated what was happening in our marriage. In the face of abuse, I didn't even consider divorce for many years because I thought that would make me a sinner.

Because of this, I allowed things in my marriage that I never fathomed I would have. I told myself that suffering in silence was better than disobeying God. I convinced myself that if I prayed harder, submitted more, forgave quicker, or endured quietly, somehow, I would change to be the wife he needed. I believed that if I could only "be better" he could find peace and would stop hurting me.

Just entertaining a small thought about divorce felt wrong. I couldn't figure out how abuse fit into the ideology that divorce was sinful. The action of abuse had to nullify that, didn't it? I had no idea. The thought didn't just feel sinful, it also felt like it would mark me as a failure. A failure at marriage, a failure as a wife, a failure as a person.

My faith, which should have been a source of freedom and truth, had been twisted into a chain that kept me bound. My viewpoint was so skewed that after many years, in my desperation to escape abuse, I even caught myself praying that he might be unfaithful so I could have what I believed was a "Biblical" reason to leave. I prayed that God would have mercy on me and spare my life by giving my husband the desire to be with another woman.

The twisted absurdity of that prayer is a testament to how trapped I felt. I was literally asking God to orchestrate a situation that would break my heart and my family just so I could have a clear path to freedom and have a "legitimate" reason to get a divorce. I was praying for another sin to be committed just so I wouldn't feel like I was a sinner. The fear and shame were so powerful that I was willing to throw away my own integrity by offering up that prayer. The irony is staggering; in a desperate search for a "Christian" way out, I was praying for my husband to commit a different sin all because I believed it was the only path to God's acceptance and my own safety.

I didn't yet understand: 1. God's heart aches when his children are abused. 2. He is protective of the vulnerable and 3. God does not call His children to stay in harm's way. Part of my struggle came from the Bible verses I heard quoted for much of my life. One of those Bible verses was Malachi 2:16: *"God hates divorce"* (NKJV). This verse felt like a command that trapped me. I wondered: *If God hates divorce, does that mean I'm sinning by wanting to flee to safety? Does God want me to endure abuse?*

After studying, I came to believe that God's heart in Malachi is not about punishing His children or excusing abuse. He is addressing the harm that comes from breaking a covenant lightly. But who had broken the covenant? Wasn't it already broken through the power and control being exercised over me? Scripture consistently emphasizes that God stands for the oppressed, that He protects the vulnerable, and that His covenant is meant to reflect love, not to be twisted into a cage of power and control. Understanding this helped me separate truth from fear. God does not want His children to remain in harm's way. Abuse is never part of His plan, and seeking safety or leaving an abusive situation does not make a person unfaithful, it honors the life God gave them. God never intended that the Bible be weaponized as a way to control a spouse (or anyone else).

This understanding gave me the courage to see a path forward. It planted the seed of realization that staying silent and enduring abuse was not what God intended for me. Speaking out was not just an act of bravery for me, it was an act of aligning with God's protection and love for me, his valued daughter, the apple of His eye.

And here's what I've learned since escaping abuse: healing starts the moment truth comes to light. Shame loses its grip when you speak up, even if your voice shakes. Telling my sister wasn't the solution to my abuse, it was the first tiny step toward freedom.

My marriage continued to implode after our beach vacation as I put my exit plan in place. The abusive behavior didn't suddenly stop. But what speaking up did was shift the power dynamic in me, it opened the first crack in the wall of silence I had built around myself for so many years.

Shame is powerful because it doesn't just attack what happened, it attacks who you are at your core. It convinces you that you're not worthy of help, love, or freedom. It doesn't just silence your voice; it suffocates your identity and convinces you that you are less than human. That's why so many women who experience abuse stay hidden, even when every part of them longs to be seen and heard.

Breaking the silence isn't just about finding the right moment or the right words, it's about pushing back against fear that overshadows your entire life. Speaking up means exposing the traumas that you have so carefully kept hidden away. It means stepping out from behind the curtain of silence and becoming vulnerable in a way you never imagined. Silence feels safer in the short term because it avoids confrontation and keeps up appearances. But silence doesn't protect, it allows the abuse to continue unchecked.

Here is the paradox: the very thing you fear most, speaking up, is also the thing that begins to set you free. The moment you allow even one trusted person to see behind the mask, shame starts to lose its grip. That's often the moment a survivor realizes they can stand up for themselves. It's empowering to hear the words come out and understand that that was the first step on a very long journey to safety and healing.

When I sent that text message, it was the first time someone else knew about my private pain. I wasn't carrying the secret alone anymore. It was scary and freeing all at the same time.

That is where healing began, in the light of truth. Courage doesn't always roar. Sometimes it's as small as sending a text with trembling hands, whispering a few words, or letting the tears fall in front of someone safe. But those small moments of courage matter more than years of self pep talks and affirmations.

When truth is spoken, shame weakens, and healing begins. Faith calls for courage, and God honors each step taken in truth. Speaking honestly begins to break the hold of fear and opens the way to the healing and freedom He intends, whether through prayer, a whispered word, or a quiet conversation. Even the smallest act of courage can be the first step toward reclaiming life and strength that has long been hidden in the shadows.

Looking back, I can clearly see the red flags that I once overlooked. I can recognize the small, subtle signs, the quiet alarms I dismissed in those very early days. Hindsight is a strange gift, it allows us to later see patterns of abuse so clearly, when years prior they were nearly invisible beneath layers of love and hope. Each tiny unsettling moment I ignored, rationalized, or excused formed a roadmap I didn't know how to read.

This reflection isn't about blame, it's about understanding. It's about seeing how easily good intentions, faith, and loyalty can be twisted into chains that keep someone trapped. And it's a reminder that awareness, clarity, education, and discernment are powerful tools, not just for surviving or preventing future pain, but for building a life in alignment with God's plan.

Chapter Gate Reminder:
The following chapter continues anonymized, paraphrased recollections intended to protect privacy.

Chapter 2: Pink Ribbons

I used to believe red flags would be obvious. I pictured bright warning lights I couldn't miss. I imagined them as shouting matches, slammed doors, and bruises. When I was a young woman, I thought surely, I would know a red flag if I saw one. But that's not how they first came. Rarely do they announce themselves with flashing lights. Instead, they slip in quietly, as soft pink ribbons, not waving red flags.

In my story, the red flags didn't start out big, they weren't explosions of anger; they were quieter things: the eye rolls that cut me down in the middle of a conversation, the demeaning and dismissive words that chipped away at my worth, the subtle rewriting of reality that left me doubting my own memory. It was his absolute certainty in *his* version of events that unsettled me most. He spoke with such conviction that I began to question myself. Surely, he had to be right... didn't he? His recollection seemed to carry so much confidence that mine began to feel uncertain.

When I dared to question his memories, he didn't have to raise his voice. A cold stare, a clenched jaw, that was enough to silence me. I usually dropped it. It wasn't worth the fight.

Even before marriage, the warning signs were there. I remember moments after we were married when he joked to others that he had started dating me young enough so he could train me the right way. He said it in front of me, like I was some eager puppy chasing the approval of her master. People laughed. I laughed too, all while the knot in my stomach grew because I was already experiencing what took place in those trainings he so casually referred to. When I look back now, I see that what he meant seemed clear, he wanted control. The message I received was that he wanted a relationship where his opinions carried the most weight, where his statements weren't challenged, and where his word stood as the final say. He didn't say "I want a submissive wife" outright, but later in the marriage, he began referencing Bible verses about submission in ways that felt out of balance. His subtle message came tucked inside his jokes and comments. The more he repeated it, the more I began to wonder if I was being too sensitive… or if something deeply wrong was taking shape right in front of me.

After I escaped, I found myself replaying the relationship in my mind. I thought about the way we interacted while we were dating, and how the warning signs crept in so quietly. What started as faint pink ribbons that I laughed at turned into blaring red sirens I had to run from. I kept asking myself, *what should I have done when I first saw those pink ribbons? Could I have stopped this from happening?* But my questions didn't stop with me. I wrestled with how to equip my children, how to help them recognize red flags in others, how to understand what healthy love looks like, and to carry into their own lives the behaviors that build safety, trust, and respect.

I had grown up in a Christian home. We prayed together. We had family worship. I had been taught values and morals from the Bible. But no one ever talked about red flags. Back then, it wasn't part of the conversation.

And yet, God *has* talked about it. Long before I knew the phrase "red flags," He gave us wisdom for recognizing the kind of people we should not tie our lives to. Let's look together at II Timothy 3:1–5 (NKJV), where Paul warns us about people who are unloving, unforgiving, slanderous, without self–control, and brutal. He ends with a clear instruction: *"from such people turn away."*

II Timothy 3:1-5 (NKJV)

"But know this, that in the last days perilous times will come: For men will be lovers of themselves, lovers of money, boasters, proud, blasphemers, disobedient to parents, unthankful, unholy, unloving, unforgiving, slanderers, without self-control, brutal, despisers of good, traitors, headstrong, haughty, lovers of pleasure rather than lovers of God, having a form of godliness but denying its power. And from such people turn away! "

Let's break down the red flags God has so clearly given us in these texts.

Lovers of Themselves

Paul begins with the phrase *"lovers of themselves."* At first glance, this sounds like basic selfishness, but it runs deeper. It's about someone so consumed with their own desires, comfort, and opinions that there's no room left for you. I believe the word "narcissist" is thrown around very casually today. But I do believe this term *"lovers of themselves"* largely encompasses what we refer to today as narcissists.

In a relationship, this can look like someone who always has things their way, what restaurant to eat at, what show to watch, how the money is spent. They need to have the last word, and their decision is immovable, no matter how practical or logical your ideas may be. At first, it may seem like they're just confident or decisive. But over time, their self-love squeezes the air out of the relationship, leaving no space for your voice or your needs.

This might be noticed in small ways at the start. Dreams, opinions, and even feelings are often minimized or dismissed as unimportant. It's very dangerous when someone believes that their wants and desires carry all the weight. A "love" that is only directed inward eventually leaves the other person unseen, unheard, and unloved.

Lovers of Money

The next warning Paul gives is *"lovers of money."* We might think of someone who is greedy or obsessed with wealth, but in relationships, this red flag often shows up as control through money, or financial abuse. It can look like a partner who uses finances to hold power, criticizing every purchase you make, keeping secrets about their spending, putting you on a minuscule allowance, or making you feel guilty for needing anything. It can look like someone not allowing their spouse to have access to any money. Credit cards, debit cards, and cash are strictly regulated. For an abuser, this is not about a budget, setting financial limits, or the bottom line in a savings account; it's about using money as a weapon.

In my personal experience, there were many times when financial decisions became completely detached from our needs and more about his wants, even though for many years, in the latter half of our marriage, I was the higher income earner. In my marriage this looked like trading in a car I absolutely loved, one that we shared, on a luxury sedan that was only for him. My name was on the car I loved. He called me while I was at work one day, letting me know he had traded our car in. But, because my name was on the trade-in, I had to go after work and sign the paperwork. When I arrived at the car dealership the sales associate made a comment about how he couldn't believe I was ok with this trade-in. He shared with me how he had heard how much I loved the car we were trading in. I didn't tell him this was all a surprise to me. Instead, I asked if I could see the car to make sure everything that I needed was out of it. The salesperson walked me to the back garage. I remember staring at the shiny black car and holding back my tears. It wasn't about the car. My tears threatened to fall because my power of choice was taken away. I didn't even know that this huge financial transaction was going to take place. And to make matters worse, my name was not on this new luxury car. And in all the years we owned it, I was only *allowed* to drive it less than a handful of times.

Money can quickly become a tool for a person that wants to control another. That's when I realized love of money isn't just dangerous to the relationship, it's dangerous to a person's soul.

Boasters

Paul then warns of *"boasters."* A boaster is someone who constantly needs to appear superior, to be seen as the smartest, strongest, or most important in the room. In dating, it might sound charming at first: endless stories of their accomplishments, the way they're always the hero in every story, never making a single mistake. You may even laugh along, feeling proud to be with someone so "impressive." But soon you realize the boasting isn't harmless when the belittling creeps in. Because the more they lift themselves up, the more they push you down.

This might show up in the way a person tells stories about the relationship. Do they make their partner the punchline, while they become the center of attention? Do they proudly share your shortcomings, whether true or false, in a way that elevates themselves in other's eyes?

Proud

Paul warns us of those who are *"proud."* Pride, in this context, isn't about healthy confidence, it's about arrogance. It's the belief that they are always right, always above correction, always superior. In a relationship, pride shows up when someone refuses to apologize, even when they're clearly wrong. It's in the way they shut down conversations by saying, *"You're overreacting,"* or *"You don't know what you're talking about."* Their pride doesn't just build themselves up, it silences you.

I remember times when I questioned his version of events, and he would look at me in a way that made me stop speaking mid-sentence. His pride didn't allow space for dialogue, only dominance. His pride kept me second-guessing myself while keeping him in the position of firm control.

Blasphemers

The next trait Paul lists is *"blasphemers."* We often think of blasphemy as taking God's name in vain, but at its root, it means using words in ways that dishonor, degrade, or distort God and His Word. In relationships, this can show up as mocking faith, belittling values, or twisting the meaning of Bible verses to chip away at your spirit. It doesn't have to sound like loud profanity; sometimes it's the whispered sarcasm, the cutting remark, or the constant stream of belittling words, or weaponizing the Bible to control someone else.

For me, it was the way Bible verses were used against me, especially towards the end of the marriage. "Wives submit to your husbands" (Ephesians 5:22 NKJV) was used, seemingly in an effort to have me bow to demands. But the next part of the text wasn't uttered: "Husbands, love your wives, just as Christ also loved the church and gave Himself for her, "(Ephesians 5:25 NKJV). God meant those words as guidance for both spouses to cherish, love, and respect each other. Instead, words that were meant to honor God were twisted into weapons of control.

Disobedient to Parents

The next one may surprise you that it made it onto Paul's list: *"disobedient to parents."* Why would Paul include this? Because how someone treats their parents often reveals how they'll treat others close to them, regardless of how old they are, or how long they have had their independence.

In relationships, this red flag shows up when someone has no respect for authority, no humility to learn from others, and no honor for those who raised them. It might look like constant complaining about their parents, refusing to listen to advice, or carrying bitterness into every interaction.

It might look like a person having contempt for their parents, like an eye roll when guidance or advice is given. It's so easy to brush these things off as normal family tension. But these things often reveal something deeper: if someone doesn't respect the ones who gave them life, how could anyone expect them to truly honor their partner?

This doesn't mean that every family has perfect parents or healthy dynamics. There's a lot of messiness in this world and there are parents that try to control their adult children. There are parents that don't value their families. There are parents that time and time again disrespect their adult children. But we always have a choice of how we respond in that moment. Sometimes we may need to walk away from family situations, sometimes strong boundaries are required. But we don't need to respond with disrespect or malice.

Unthankful

An "*unthankful*" spirit is one that cannot see the good, no matter how much is given. In a relationship, this looks like constant criticism, an inability to acknowledge effort, and a refusal to express gratitude. Instead of appreciating small acts of love, service, or sacrifice, the unthankful person focuses only on what is missing in a relationship or an interaction. An unthankful person continually asks "what about me?" instead of working to build a relationship that's mutually beneficial. Over time, this drains the joy out of giving and creates an atmosphere where nothing feels good enough.

In today's world, it may sound like sarcasm, constant complaints, or the belief that their partner should always be doing more. Scripture reminds us in 1 Thessalonians 5:18 to *"give thanks in everything,"* but someone marked by ingratitude is blind to blessings and quick to tear down rather than build up.

Unholy

To be *"unholy"* is to disregard, or treat lightly, what God calls holy. This isn't just about church attendance, it's about the condition of the heart. It's not just about obvious sins; it's a mindset that places self above God.

In relationships, this can show up as disregard for moral boundaries, disrespect for others' values, or a lifestyle that prioritizes selfish desires over integrity. Today, it might look like someone who excuses lying, manipulates others for gain, or mocks Godly behavior. They make their own rules and expect others to comply, leaving no room for accountability or reverence for God's standards.

In relationships, unholiness can show up in the way someone treats their vows, their body, or their word. It's living as though nothing is sacred, not faith, not marriage, not integrity. It can look like promises broken without remorse and boundaries crossed without hesitation.

Unloving

Paul warns of people who are *"without natural affection"*, this is a chilling description of hearts grown cold. This trait points to a rejection of what is right and pure. In modern terms, it appears in partners who not only refuse to show love but also belittle kindness or undermine virtues like humility and generosity. They may dismiss acts of service or treat ethical boundaries as trivial. When someone can't or won't show love, they subtly erode your sense of value.

Love is patient, kind, and nurturing. But unloving people withdraw warmth and replace it with control or apathy. It's the silent treatment used as punishment. It's affection dangled like a prize to be earned.

It's the absence of genuine care for your well-being. I remember craving tenderness, kind words, a gentle touch. Instead, what I often felt was distance, indifference, and affection withheld. That absence was its own kind of wound.

Unforgiving

Some translations call this *"irreconcilable."* It's the refusal to let go of offenses, even small ones. In toxic relationships, past mistakes are stored like ammunition, ready to be fired when needed. We all make mistakes, but when someone keeps a permanent record of your wrongs, it becomes a weapon. An unforgiving person will remind you of your past failures every time they want to win an argument or keep you small. Instead of extending grace, they hold your history against you. True forgiveness doesn't mean excusing sin or allowing the same sin to keep occurring. It does mean refusing to chain someone to their past. When forgiveness is withheld, connection is replaced with guilt, and a relationship built on guilt can never thrive. When forgiveness is missing, control and condemnation can very easily take its place.

Slanderers

This word means *"false accusers,"* but it's also tied to gossip, twisting the truth, and speaking words meant to destroy. In abusive relationships, slander may come in the form of mocking you, destroying your character to others, making you the punchline of cruel jokes, or flat-out lying about you to shift blame away from themselves. Words wound deeply, and when someone consistently uses their tongue to cut, it's not harmless, it's a warning sign.

But in intimate relationships, slander doesn't just happen in public, it also happens behind closed doors. It's the whisper that *you're crazy,* and the stories told to you that make you question your own thoughts and memories. It's the comments that subtly undermine your credibility to others, but also within your own mind.

Without Self-Control

Lack of self-control doesn't always look like rage or addictions, though it can. Sometimes it looks like someone who refuses to take responsibility, who lets their emotions dictate their every response. Sometimes it shows up as reckless spending. And sometimes it means they explode over small inconveniences, or they lash out when challenged. They justify reckless decisions by blaming others for their choices. Nothing is ever their fault. When someone lacks self-control, you end up living in a constant state of unpredictability with a target that is constantly moving and consequences when you can't hit the bullseye of their expectations.

A person without self-control may not always look dangerous at first, but given time, their lack of restraint will bleed into every area of life. Their rage may simmer just beneath the surface, waiting for the smallest spark. This looks like a spouse in a constant state of stress, learning to walk on eggshells, to predict and prevent explosions. But no matter how careful someone is, they can never control what someone else refuses to master in themselves.

Brutal

Brutality doesn't always mean physical violence. It can mean harsh words, cruel sarcasm, or emotional punishment. Brutality is the opposite of gentleness, it crushes instead of comforts. This word is strong for a reason. Brutality is cruelty, the absence of tenderness. What makes this different from "without self-control" is the deliberate, intentional efforts to cause harm. It doesn't always start with physical harm, it can begin with verbal assaults, with cold and cutting tones. Brutality thrives on intimidation, the fear of what might come next.

If they can keep you feeling smaller, weaker, or constantly afraid of how they'll respond, that's not love, that's brutality. Words sometimes cut deeper than any physical blow ever could. Words that mock worth, belittle faith, and minimize pain can cut worse than any knife and leave bruises deep within a soul.

Despisers of Good

This trait reveals a heart that mocks or resents what is pure and good. Instead of celebrating truth, kindness, or faithfulness, they find ways to criticize or corrupt it. It's those who roll their eyes at purity, who scoff at kindness, who mock integrity. In relationships, this might look like someone tearing down your desire to go to church, belittling your faith, or ridiculing you for pursuing godly friendships. When someone despises what is good, they will slowly try to pull you away from it.

When I tried to live by my faith, it often felt unwelcome or misunderstood, even though he professed to be a Christian. Moments of joy or spiritual growth were often met with sarcasm or dismissal. When I believed that God had worked out something in my life I would share it with my husband. His responses would try to minimize my belief in God's intervention. I was met with a response that told me God didn't care what happened in my life and that God doesn't perform miracles today. He dismissed them as unimportant. His contempt for goodness made me question whether joy and goodness were ever given a place in our home.

Traitors, Headstrong, Haughty

These three come as a cluster. A traitor betrays trust, whether in big or small ways. In relationships, betrayal can be physical, emotional, or spiritual. It can mean broken promises, secrets kept, or loyalty sold for selfish gain. Headstrong means recklessness, driven by impulse instead of wisdom. Haughty means arrogant, looking down on others. Together, these qualities create instability, disloyalty, and pride. A person like this will abandon you when it suits them, bulldoze over your feelings, and make you feel "less than."

The sting of betrayal can come in both subtle and blatant ways. Things shared in confidence thrown back in anger. Commitments broken without hesitation. Each betrayal reinforces the message: *you cannot trust me.* It looks like someone disregarding their partner's voice, concerns, or family's needs. Their way was the only way. And no one should ever dare to question them. They paint you as the enemy. Their haughtiness appears in the way they speak about you to others, as though you are naïve, less capable, less intelligent. In private, it can be even worse. Haughtiness makes you feel small, not because you are, but because someone else insists on towering over you.

Lovers of Pleasure Rather than Lovers of God

This characteristic cuts deep. When pleasure becomes the pursuit, God is pushed aside. A person who loves pleasure more than God will choose what feels good over what is right, what brings comfort over what requires sacrifice. They may say the right words, but their actions reveal where their heart truly lies. This doesn't just mean indulgence in obvious sins; it means a life centered on self rather than surrender to God.

In relationships, this looks like someone who values comfort, fun, or gratification over commitment, sacrifice, or obedience to God's Word. This shows itself through spiritual matters that are dismissed as irrelevant and choices are made to please self rather than honor God.

A Form of Godliness Without Its Power

Paul concludes this list with the most powerful, and concerning, characteristic of all. People that have *"a form of godliness but deny its power."* In other words, they may look religious, they may even go to church, hold a position of leadership, quote Scripture, or say the right things, but their lives don't reflect Christ.

This is one of the hardest things to reconcile. Someone outwardly appearing to be spiritual, knowing just the right words to say in public, holding just the right church offices. But when doors are closed, love, joy, peace, patience, and kindness are rarely visible. There was form, but no power.

And the final command is sobering: *"From such people turn away."*

* * * * * * * * * * * * * *

Abuse rarely begins with violence or overt threats. It starts quietly, almost imperceptibly, in ways that seem minor or easily dismissible. But these behaviors lay the groundwork for deeper control. Over time, small acts of disrespect, manipulation, or dismissal escalate into intimidation, threats, and sometimes physical harm. Recognizing these early patterns is critical because, if we don't, they are the breadcrumbs leading us down a path to greater danger. These are the signs that something is fundamentally wrong long before a crisis emerges.

It's easy to rationalize minor infractions, chalking them up to a bad day or stress at work. It's even easy to laugh off the stories that demean us, and sometimes, someone else. But each "small" incident chips away at self-esteem, rewrites boundaries, and normalizes behavior that should never be tolerated. Ignoring these early warning signs gives the abuser more power, allowing patterns to solidify and the cycle of control to tighten. What feels trivial in the moment can, over time, become the invisible cage that traps a person emotionally, mentally, and spiritually. The key is to notice, acknowledge, and trust your instincts before the subtle pink ribbon behaviors escalate into something far more dangerous.

Looking back, it's easy to see the warning signs I missed, the subtle ways that control crept into my life, and the traits I now recognize in hindsight. But identifying red flags is only the first step. Understanding how these abusers operate, often in a deliberate pattern to control, truly shines a light on abuse. In the next chapter, we will take a closer look at power and control, a tactic that abusers use to dominate, confuse, and silence their partners. Understanding the elements of power and control helped me connect the dots in my own story and begin to understand that what I experienced wasn't random, it was a calculated pattern, one that God's truth calls us to recognize and resist.

Chapter Gate Reminder:
The following chapter continues anonymized, paraphrased recollections intended to protect privacy.

Chapter 3: The Rulebook

Shortly after we married, the air inside our house began to feel so thick I could barely breathe. It carried an unspoken heaviness, like the quiet before a storm. My stomach stayed knotted, my body tense, bracing for the next moment of tension that might come from the smallest perceived slight. Over the years, I began to sense what was expected of me: perfection in my appearance, in our home, in our children. I was supposed to contribute financially, but never in a way that outpaced him. And when I did outpace him, I had to go along with the illusion that he made more money than I did when we spoke to our friends and family.

His idea of perfection seemed to shift constantly, always just out of reach. It felt like there was a rulebook for our life together, one that I was never allowed to read, but still had to strictly follow. Every sudden sound made me flinch; every unexpected silence unsettled me. And serving as a buffer between him and the children became its own kind of exhaustion.

I once read a book that introduced the idea of "cognitive reframing." The book instructed wives that were frustrated or demeaned in their marriage to consciously visualize a different image about her husband. She was instructed to view his behaviors in a different light so that her emotional and physical response would change toward him. Instead of focusing on negative thoughts, the wife was supposed to actively re-evaluate situations and reframe them so she could replace her feelings with more positive thoughts. According to the book, the process was not intended to have women lie to themselves, but to have them pull the positive moments out of otherwise negative situations. I was desperate to try anything that might help. I thought maybe, just maybe, if I changed my mindset, I could change my marriage. So, each night, as I laid my head on the pillow I would pray and ask for God's help. I would go over all the things in my mind that had happened, both good and bad, then I would intentionally focus on only the positive interactions with my husband. Sometimes I didn't have a single positive thing from that day, and I would need to mentally go back to positive interactions that happened a few days prior. But each night, as I worked to view my life in a different light, sleep evaded me. As much as I tried to reframe things, I still felt like I had to keep one eye open to protect my children and myself.

The bulk of my husband's anger and control was directed at me. But his frustrations bubbled over onto our children, mainly our son, from the time they were very young. There were unwritten and ever-changing rules for them as well. Our son had delayed speech, but when he finally spoke, he had the vocabulary of a much older child. He still had some challenges with his speech, which made him say some words in the cutest way. When he was about three years old, he couldn't say the hard C sounds in words like car or catch. He would pronounce it as a T, and sometimes an S sound instead. I still remember so clearly that night after dinner when his sister asked for a cookie. Her father happily handed her some. Then my son asked for a cookie too. He said it in the cutest way with the biggest smile on his face. It was the sweetest request from an innocent little boy sitting on his booster seat. What happened next broke something in me. I clearly remember my husband telling my son he couldn't have

38

a cookie until he said the word correctly. I watched my son try again, but the same adorable pronunciation came out. I saw the confusion in his eyes when his request was denied. He was only three, still learning, yet his father told him until he could say the words correctly, he wouldn't get a cookie.

I saw the tears in my son's eyes and the confusion on his face. At only three he seemed to know that he couldn't say the words in the way his father wanted him to. But that was how things functioned in our home; it was his way or no way. My daughter sat frozen at the table. She and her brother are very close in age, and she was too little to understand the dynamics of what was happening in front of her. But she was visibly stunned, remaining completely still with an unbitten cookie in her hand. My anger bubbled up in a way that I didn't want to stop, but I knew I needed to hide my feelings to keep the situation calm. My children had not seen the abuse yet, and I didn't want them to see it that night, or any other night. But I knew if I didn't stand up in that moment for my son it would turn into a snowball effect, and he would never feel safe. I walked over to the island and grabbed two lemon Oreos out of the package. I calmly turned to my son, twisted the Oreos apart, just like he liked them, and laid them creamy side up in front of him. "Here you go Bub" I said with a smile. I breathed a sigh of relief as my husband walked into the other room.

Later that night, after reading the kids their bedtime story and tucking them in with extra kisses, I headed downstairs. My husband was waiting for me. I can still remember feeling uneasy as I came down the steps and saw his stiff posture. His arms were bent at the elbows in sharp right angles. His fingertips pressed together, forming a steeple. I had seen this stance before. When I got to the bottom of the stairs, he gestured sharply toward the open door, motioning me inside, and I obeyed.

When I stepped through the door, everything happened in a blur. I remember the shock of being grabbed, the sting of the skin twisting on my arm, and the terror that stiffened every muscle in my body from head to toe. I still recall the spit hitting my face, being shoved backward and hitting the floor hard. For a moment, everything went dark. When I opened my eyes, the back of my head was against the side of the desk. Pain radiated through my head. I was dizzy and disoriented. The throbbing pain pulsed through my head, the worst headache I had ever experienced.

I recall seeing him standing at my feet, slowly coming into focus. I don't remember much about what he said after I woke up, but the gist of his words was to never go against him. I wanted to grab my children and run so far away he would never find us, never hurt us again.

But I stayed. I stayed because fear had settled deep inside me, fear of what could happen to the children when they were with him if I wasn't there, fear of what he might do if I left, fear of being condemned by others for walking away. I was afraid if I divorced him that I would be labeled a sinner. Fear created invisible walls that kept me captive.

****

I want to pause here. It is extremely important to highlight that abuse is not limited to physical violence. It often begins with control, isolation, or the slow erosion of self-worth. According to the National Domestic Violence Hotline, abuse can take many forms: physical, emotional, sexual, financial, digital, or psychological. It can look like manipulation, humiliation, intimidation, or using faith, children, or finances as tools of control.

For anyone reading this who recognizes parts of their own life in these words, you are not alone, and what is happening is not your fault. If you are in immediate danger, please call 911. If you are not in immediate danger, but need to connect with resources, there is a resource page located at the back of this book. If you are struggling to connect with the right resource, please reach out to me through the contact tab on my web page. This page is monitored, and we can help you connect with the right resources for your situation.

****

Nearly twenty years into the relationship, the rules for me had multiplied. These rules weren't written down anywhere. There were definitely rules that I knew so well, rules that I could recite by heart, while others seemed to appear out of thin air. There were rules that determined how long I could be away from home and what friends I could have. There were rules about who I could talk to on the phone when I was at home (family included), what time I was required to get off work each day, what time I had to have dinner on the table each night, and extremely rigid rules for the children's bedtime routines. Some rules changed without warning, keeping me in a constant state of uncertainty and working to anticipate when the rules might change based on his mood.

It was like living in a game whose instructions were rewritten daily, and the penalties for one wrong move could be severe. I learned to read every expression, every sigh, every subtle shift in the air. I became fluent in anticipating danger before it arrived. My days revolved around trying to remember every instruction he had given me while my nights revolved around silent prayers for peace and safety.

When I broke one of these invisible rules, even unknowingly, there was always a consequence waiting for me. Sometimes consequences came through silent treatment that stretched for days; other times consequences were words that left bruises long after the anger stopped. But the hardest consequence of all was the erosion of identity, the quiet unraveling that happens when you start believing the lie that you deserve it.

I tried harder and harder to follow every rule, hoping that maybe, this time, it would be enough to keep the peace. But peace built on fear is not real. In that season, I desperately tried to cling to the small pieces of truth that reminded me I still belonged to God. But the more time that passed the more the fog rolled in that clouded my view of what God wanted in my life. There were still moments when I sensed God's presence. Those moments of stillness came when I could hold my children, feel their warm hugs, or hear them tell me they loved me. It was in those moments where I could feel God's presence and hear His whisper of his protection and provision in my life.

Isaiah 61:1 (NKJV) says, "He has sent Me to heal the brokenhearted, to proclaim liberty to the captives." That verse became more than just words on a page to me; they gave me a small peak into the heart of God. Though I didn't yet understand how freedom would come, I began to believe that God's promises were still for me, even in the middle of my invisible captivity.

Over time, I eventually came to realize that the rulebook governing our lives had no end. Each chapter was written with the pen of control, revised in silence, and enforced without mercy. No matter how carefully I tried to follow the rules, the finish line kept moving.

Still, even in that perpetual pattern of uncertainty, something in me refused to stop rising. Every morning, I got up and kept going for my two beautiful children. I genuinely smiled for them, packed lunches, attended parent/teacher meetings, read bedtime stories, and prayed over them while they slept. They were the reasons I continued to push through the heaviness each day. They were the reasons I still believed that a different kind of life was possible.

Once I realized that the rulebook existed, I tried to accommodate it, appease him, and keep the peace. But after living under unreasonable rules and the nonstop changes to the rules, I didn't want to just survive the rulebook, I wanted to take the book completely out of circulation, so my children could grow up free from fear.

And so, quietly, almost imperceptibly, the first thoughts of what safety might look like began to take shape.

Chapter Gate Reminder:
The following chapter continues anonymized, paraphrased recollections intended to protect privacy.

Chapter 4: Safety Planning

I did not know the term *safety planning* back then. What I did know was fear. It was not just the fear of bruises or broken bones; it was the fear planted deep in my heart with the sentiments that so easily fell from his mouth. He told me, in very severe words, that I will paraphrase here, that if I ever left him, he would not rest until he saw me lying face-down in a ditch without a penny to my name. Yes, these things hurt me deeply, how could he think of these things, let alone speak them aloud? BUT, by the time these ugly sentiments were shared with me, I was hearing his veiled threats and put-downs for so many years that they almost became expected. Although the general expectation of veiled threats was there, the sentiment still stung my heart. The echo of his words lingered in my thoughts and left deep hurts that no one could see.

Once I stopped visibly reacting to the threats against me, showing that the tactics did not hold as much weight any longer, the topic was shifted to the one subject that still could affect me: the kids. I remember him saying that if I ever left him, I would never see my kids again. I did not ask him what that meant, but I always wondered: was he planning to keep me from my children? Or could this be an even more serious threat? I tried to keep my expressions neutral when he would say things like this, but I do not think I was very successful.

Threatening me through my children was the biggest mistake that could ever be made. I finally realized I had to stand up. I needed to be more intentional, more cautious, and so much more planned in the process. Words threatening to keep me from my children were his weapon of choice, more powerful than any hand ever raised to me. These inferences played over and over in my mind like a song stuck on repeat. I did not yet call it a plan, but little by little, I began gathering scraps of courage, stitching them together into a strategy for escaping.

****

What I quickly learned was that safety planning cannot be done as a one-size-fits-all approach. Every person's situation is different, and the details are both complex and deeply personal. For one woman, it might mean immediately finding a safe place to stay, while for another it could mean months of careful preparation. It means going through her entire life with a fine-tooth comb to ensure that not one aspect is missed. For some, it even means teaching their children age-appropriate tasks that they can do in an emergency.

There are so many layers of safety planning that most people never think about until they are in the middle of it. It involves coordination of housing, transportation, electronics, finances, and legal protections. But it also involves planning for emotional and spiritual safety. It means learning how to rebuild trust in yourself after being conditioned to doubt every decision. It's not just about escaping danger but about laying out a foundation for what comes next.

****

My safety planning did not happen all at once, at the end of the marriage. It began quite a few years before the actual separation, in small, almost imperceptible steps. At first, my efforts were for my husband, an attempt to calm the storm that seemed to be constantly in his heart. I begged him to move our children out of an urban area to a more rural area, somewhere safer, slower paced. Somewhere that the newspaper was not publishing weekly reports about knives and guns being brought to the school our children would eventually attend. I thought maybe, just maybe, a change of scenery, and living closer to some very dear friends, would ease the tension that constantly seemed to simmer beneath the surface. I did not yet realize that these early decisions made to placate him were the first steps in quietly shaping the foundation of an eventual escape.

Early one Sunday morning as we lay in bed, the sun was just peeking through the skylight. We talked about how we were both ready to move. We were ready to have a slower paced life in a quiet town far from where we currently live. I was so happy I could barely contain myself! This would have to relieve some of his stress! I told myself this would give us the fresh start we needed, a new foundation on which we could build a healthy relationship. My plan had to work; it needed to work. Failure was not an option.

Moving across the country lifted some of life's pressures, at first. And for a short while things felt normal, normal in the sense of what I had imagined a healthy marriage to be. We were working to build a new life together. I clung to the hope that this fresh start would finally give us a different kind of life. But that illusion did not last long. We carried our unspoken baggage with us, and it wasn't long before the same patterns of control resurfaced. When the physical abuse returned, the weight of reality sank in. I knew my dream of peace was gone. That's when I understood I needed a different kind of plan: not just for survival in the marriage, but for escape.

I began tucking away tiny amounts of cash in my desk at work and memorizing phone numbers and addresses of my family and friends, just in case. I silently mapped the routes we might take to flee the house. I rehearsed escape scenarios repeatedly in my head in case we needed to leave in a rush. I no longer hung my car keys on the hook by the door; I kept them in my backpack so they couldn't be taken or hidden from me. That lesson was learned after it happened for the first time. I carried a mental list of safe people and places we could run to if the worst happened. I knew I could not sit idly by and wait for the unthinkable to happen. I had to be ready, we had to be ready, because deep down I believed the threats spoken to me would one day become reality.

It was my kids who finally gave me the courage to leave. I had never been able to summon that strength for myself, but the mama bear in me woke up the moment my children became witnesses. Their safety outweighed everything else. I knew I had to show them, by my actions, that abuse is never acceptable, that no one has the right to harm another, and that it should never be tolerated or repeated. Protecting them became my mission, and with that came a clarity and determination I had never known before.

I set a promise in stone: I would leave under one of two circumstances, either once I completed my degree, trusting that education would open doors to stability and opportunity for the three of us, or if my children ever saw the abuse firsthand. That was the line I refused to let him cross. No matter what I endured, I would not allow my children to be caught in the crosshairs.

Juggling a full-time job while pushing hard to finish my degree was my daily reality. The bachelor's program I enrolled in met only two nights a week, from 6:00 to 10:00, with the remaining coursework completed online. Although that structure was difficult because of my home life, it was also a schedule that allowed me to keep working while still being present with my children most evenings.

Just a handful of classes stood between me and my degree. The finish line was finally in sight, and with that diploma the chance for a different life, a safer life would come. I was so close I could almost taste it. Not only was my degree within reach, but my safety plan was nearly complete.

Just the act of planning our exit gave me a courage I had not felt in years. A quiet peace settled over me, subtle but unmistakable, as if a small light had been switched on in a room long shrouded in darkness. Part of that planning was learning to move carefully through the house, staying as silent as possible, following the schedule that was developed for me to the letter, smiling whenever he entered the room, and never letting my face show that the words meant as daggers didn't break the skin any longer. I was trying to keep his anger at bay while quietly plotting our path to freedom.

But just as freedom felt within reach, the very line I had sworn I would never let him cross was shattered. That night my children saw what had previously been kept behind the mask.

I still recall that night so clearly. My husband walked into the kitchen and leaned against the peninsula, silently watching. The kids and I were busy pulling together toppings for taco salad: shredding cheese, pouring chips into a bowl, setting the table. I moved the chili from the crockpot to the table, and the only thing left to do was chop the onions. That was when he finally spoke. He said something about me cutting the onions wrong and that I needed to curl my fingers against the knife blade. I remember him continuing his chiding of me by saying something to the effect of him being tired of having to manage me all the time.

I was exhausted from walking on eggshells, from the constant orders, from being treated like I couldn't do anything right, not even cut the onions. I was sick of being bullied. In that moment, I could not recall the last kind word or gentle gesture he had shown me. Something in me finally said *enough is enough*. With disdain written across my face, I shot back, "Why don't you come show me how it's done?"

I even surprised myself with my reply to him. This tone was new from me. I was always so careful not to provoke him, especially in front of the children. His response was immediate, like a roar. I recognized the look on his face, and I knew in my heart what was coming next. I felt my stomach turn and I knew I needed to leave the kitchen before my children witnessed what I expected would come next.

I had worked for years to hide the abuse from my children. I needed to protect their little eyes and ears from the ugliness. That evening, I just knew that if I did not leave the kitchen immediately, that what I had worked to hide would be exposed. I knew my children would learn first-hand what had previously been happening in secret.

Instinct took over. I rushed from the kitchen, trying to make it to the next room so the children would not see what I feared would come next. But the next thing I remember is hearing heavy footsteps behind me, feeling that sharp sudden pain in the middle of my back, and falling forward. I went down hard, face-first on the hallway floor.

Pain shot through my arm as I tried to break the fall. I felt so small as I lay there on the cold wood floor. I still recall the yelling, but I cannot recall the words being used. It was too much to process in that moment. At my feet, my daughter stood crying. I felt his attention turn towards our daughter and I fully believed he was going to hurt her. I reached for his pants' leg, clinging to it with all I had left, and pleaded with the kids to run and lock themselves in her bedroom.

As the kids ran, I prayed desperately: *"Lord, protect them."* These were the only words I could find to pray. My brain shifted into neutral as the shock of the events set in.

As I lay there on the floor of the hallway, I heard my daughter's bedroom door close. I closed my eyes, clenching every muscle in my body, bracing for what might come next. I heard the sound of keys jingling. I heard the door into the garage open. I heard the car door slam and the big garage door roll up and back down again. The silence that followed was deafening. Slowly, painfully, I pushed myself upright and leaned back against the wall, trying to collect my scattered thoughts. That was it; my line had been crossed. What was I going to say to my kids? How was I going to tell them mommy and daddy were divorcing? They had already figured out we were sleeping in separate bedrooms, but how much did they really understand?

My mind raced through the days ahead: Our daughter was leaving for camp in just over a week, then our family vacation was scheduled right after her return, and then our son's camp would follow. I forced myself to breathe, to think logically, to map out how we might survive until then. I should have packed up all of our stuff and left right then. But my mind still was not fully comprehending the danger we were in, and I wanted to minimize the upheaval the kids were about to go through. Once I had a few things organized in my mind, I climbed the stairs to check on the kids.

I knocked softly on my daughter's door. "Guys, it's Mom. Dad went out for a little while." She opened the door but immediately closed it again, locking it behind me. She walked over to sit next to her brother on the floor at the end of her bed. I sat across from them, the weight of the moment pressing down on all three of us.

I remember the words my daughter shared that day, her words cut straight through me. She wondered why we were still there, why we hadn't left.

My preteen daughter had more clarity than I did. She knew, in ways I had not yet fully realized, that what was happening was not right. Later, I learned she had seen and heard things before. That night was not the first time she had witnessed what I had tried so hard to hide. She later shared that what she saw that night wasn't even the worst thing she had witnessed. She told me things that made me cry. I was filled with tremendous guilt because I had fooled myself into thinking that what I had endured was being kept a secret from my children. Their young minds had been forced to understand far more than their years should have ever demanded.

I had promised myself so many times that I was going to make a better life for the three of us, away from harm. But it was the events of that evening that finally put my plans into motion. I didn't know what I was doing. I didn't know who to ask for help, or even if I should ask for help. I believed that if I canceled our family vacation, he would only make the divorce even more difficult, so I resolved to wait through my daughter's camp, the vacation, and then my son's camp. It was an extremely dangerous choice that I made. My guess is that as you read this, you are shaking your head asking, "Why didn't you leave right then?" It is a valid question. I know now that this choice was a huge mistake. It was gravely dangerous. I had been living in this nightmare for so many years that it became *almost* normal. And this decision was made using the tools I had in my emotional toolbox at the time.

During that window of time, when I was waiting to implement our escape plan, was when the office incident happened. The time when I knew the suffocation was very real and I thought my life was over. It was a brutal awakening, one that I am so grateful to have survived. If I had the chance to do it over again, I would leave sooner. But hindsight is always 20/20.

In the days that followed, I mentally built and rebuilt my safety plan. I felt fairly confident my phone was not being used to track my location since it came through work, and no one else ever had access to it. I checked my car for recording devices, just to make sure no one could listen in on any conversations I was having about escaping. I quietly opened a new bank account in my name alone and spoke with Human Resources about rerouting my direct deposit. The timing had to be exact; I needed to make the switch without raising alarms when the paycheck suddenly stopped showing up in our joint account. Every move had to be careful, calculated, and invisible.

He knew that the *official* separation was coming, one where we were no longer living under the same roof in separate bedrooms. He told me that after the separation of our households, he should still be in charge of our finances, that we could still have joint accounts. He even implied that we could still have shared credit cards. He said it would work best that way. The reality had not set in for him yet that he was no longer in control of me, my finances, or the decisions I made for my life.

I called a realtor friend and started looking at houses. He did too. This was good! He seemed to finally accept the fact that we needed to plan for separate futures. Our house was for sale, but no one had looked at it yet. The price was way too high, well above comparable houses on the market, but he would not hear a word about listing the house at a price that better reflected the comparables or the price that the realtor recommended. I wondered if this was to keep us stuck, unable to purchase anything separately because we had the burden of a mortgage weighing us down.

I was still fooling myself into thinking that things were slowly coming together. We were still separated under the same roof, but I could handle it for a while, or so I thought. At least with the way things were in that moment I could pretend he was accepting the inevitable. There was light at the end of the tunnel. For the moment, we were coexisting in a fragile kind of peace, the house unnervingly calm.

No one should have to do this alone. Coming alongside someone as they build a safety plan is one of the most precious forms of support you can offer. It is not about taking control or deciding for them; it is about listening, encouraging, and helping them think through the steps that will keep them safe, both physically and emotionally. It may mean helping them work through the actual plan, offering to store a bag of essentials, driving them to an appointment, helping them find community resources, or simply being the person they can call when the fear feels too heavy to carry alone.

After the text I sent to one of my sisters as I sat on the beach, I stayed silent until I got back from that vacation. Once I was home, I called my sisters, one by one, and shared with them about the mess that had been my marriage for many years. I called my best friend and shared it with her. I needed people to know what was happening. I needed people to watch out for me. I needed someone to listen, to be a voice of reason in the middle of my brain fog.

Helping someone plan for safety is a touchy ground. It requires patience, discernment, and respect for the survivor's choices. You are not rescuing, pushing, or trying to convince them to leave. You are walking with them toward safety. Thankfully, this is what these amazing women in my life did for me.

Safety planning is the quiet, strategic work of someone who is refusing to be trapped any longer, who is reclaiming their right to live free from harm. For those stuck in abuse, safety planning can be the bridge between danger and survival, between despair and the first glimmer of hope. It is not just about leaving; it is about living.

Shortly after my divorce was finalized, I learned the term for the plans I had made, "safety planning." It was a Saturday afternoon when I got a call from a friend inviting me to lunch with her and her husband the following day. When we met at the restaurant on Sunday afternoon, we exchanged big hugs. I was so happy to see them and catch up on everything that was happening in life. As we settled into a big booth, they both became so serious. They shared with me that my ex-husband was making threatening statements towards me. They were shocked when he made statements saying if he couldn't have me, no one would. I was not surprised. It didn't even really phase me. I was already on high alert, but at least now I had other people who were aware of his behaviors and personally heard the statements. I believed he was using these friends to get his message back to me. Through them, he was able to communicate with me without making statements directly to me or putting anything in writing. Threats were not new to me; those happened throughout our marriage, but learning about statements being made about me to other people was the newest form of those threats.

Later that day I went online and searched for an organization that could help someone stay safe after a divorce from an abusive spouse. I had heard of the National Domestic Violence Hotline, but I had never used their services. I read on their website that one of the things they help with is setting up a safety plan. So, I called the hotline, not even sure how to ask for help or what information to share with them. The woman on the phone shared with me how they can help. She said they could assist with a plan that keeps someone safe while they are still in the home and planning an exit; they can also help a survivor connect with resources for the exit, and they can assist with a post-exit plan. This was when I first realized that even though I was already divorced, I still needed a safety plan. I did not know where to begin.

The woman on their hotline walked me through several aspects of the post-exit safety plan. She said if I could afford cameras or a security system that would help me. I already had a few cheap cameras I bought online, so I felt that would suffice for now, since I did not have the funds for anything more. But the biggest aha moment for me was when she said I needed to journal absolutely everything that I could. She said I needed to write down details of every abusive incident from as far back as I could remember, listing the dates of each occurrence, to the best of my recollection. She instructed me to be as thorough as possible in my journaling, documenting every small detail of my memories of each event. She said I needed to share that document with someone I trusted and instruct that person if anything happened to me, they should share the file with the police.

I felt numb. Her words were a huge wake up call. I had deluded myself into thinking that after we left, we would be safe. I fully believed my children and I would have peace. I never, in a million years, thought that I would have to journal about everything that had happened and was still happening in my life. It was a shock that all this journaling was a safeguard, in case I lost my life, so that the police would have some idea of the history of all the sordid details. I ended that call both grateful and shaken. I realized that leaving was not the end of the danger, only the beginning of learning how to live differently. Each step from then on would require vigilance, wisdom, and faith. This was a kind of survival I had never imagined.

That conversation forced me to face a painful truth: safety was not something that magically appeared after leaving. It had to be built, layer by layer, through every cautious step and prayerful decision. Survival was about choosing life for myself and my children and choosing to believe that God still had more for us than fear and hiding.

I still had so many questions about my faith, and what God says about marriage, divorce, and abuse. There were many times that faith carried me through some very dark moments, but also times when my beliefs were tangled up with fear, shame, and submission. In the next chapter we will follow that thread: untangling the truth of God's heart from the lies told and understanding the path to find faith that frees rather than binds.

NOTE: The actual act of safety planning is something that cannot be covered in this book. Safety planning takes a lot of care and diligence that requires much more intricate training than what can be provided in this book. If you are in immediate danger, please call the emergency line specific to your location (in the United States that number is 911). For non-emergency issues, if you can safely call the National Domestic Violence Hotline, their contact information is listed on the Resource page at the end of this book. They can assist you with safety planning. Connecting with an advocate in your local area is extremely beneficial. If you do not know how to connect with an advocate in your area, I am happy to help you make that connection. Please contact me through the contact page on my website listed at the end of the Resource page.

If you are trying to help someone develop a safety plan, a resource will be published on the www.UntangledJourney.com website in December of 2025 to help you walk through the safety planning process. You will be able to find that resource on my webpage listed at the back of the book.

Chapter Gate Reminder:
The following chapter continues anonymized, paraphrased recollections intended to protect privacy.

Chapter 5: Faith Untangled

I can still picture myself sitting in church as a young teenager, my eyes wandering up toward the ceiling covered in wooden slats and thick beams. The pendulum lights swaying ever so slightly overhead. The pastor was preaching on the seventh commandment: *"Thou shalt not commit adultery"* (Exodus 20:14 NKJV). He was not a particularly engaging speaker, but that morning his words were sharp and unmistakable. He spoke of the seriousness of adultery and declared that God hated divorce for any reason other than infidelity. Even as a young girl, I knew why he had chosen that topic. The rumors about a few couples in our congregation separating had already spread, and this sermon was intended to be more than a lesson for the church; it was a warning shot.

I remember the car ride home just as vividly. My parents spoke quietly about how sad it was that these marriages were ending. They talked about the consequences: how those individuals would no longer be allowed to serve in church leadership roles, no longer welcome to sing in the choir, no longer seen in the same light within the church. I sat in the back seat, unusually silent. Normally I was chatty, always quick to fill the space with laughter or questions, but that day I just listened. I absorbed every word, letting the weight of their conversation and the pastor's message sink in.

From the time I was young, I was taught to believe that divorce simply was not an option. In the church circles I grew up in, the only acceptable reason for divorce was infidelity, and even then, it should be walked into with extreme caution and only if the unfaithful spouse refused to repent. Any other reason for divorce was labeled as a sin on the part of the person that filed the papers. That message sank deep into me, shaping not just how I thought about marriage, but what I expected of myself and eventually, what I believed that I was supposed to endure so I could be a *good* Christian wife.

When my ex-husband and I were engaged we still lived in separate cities. We planned a weekend to travel to see my parents. We arrived on a Friday afternoon. That evening my dad read something out of the Bible for family worship. My parents sat with us for a while, talking about our upcoming marital vows and the importance of how we should treat each other. My dad's demeanor turned from his normal joking to a serious admonition to my fiancé. My Dad told him that I needed to be protected and treated well, and of course my fiancé agreed.

My mom and dad said goodnight and headed upstairs. My fiancé and I stayed talking in the living room. It's a memory that, when I close my eyes, it is still so vivid. We were sitting on the cream-colored velour sofa with a ruffle all around the bottom. It's a style that would sell now as "vintage." I still remember the smell of that velour sofa as we talked late into the night. We talked about what we wanted our marriage to look like. We both agreed, without hesitation, "Divorce is not an option." At the time, those words were sincere; they felt strong and noble, like a safeguard that would anchor us through whatever storms might come. I genuinely believed that we could conquer anything together. We were so young (in our early 20s) and had not experienced much in life yet. We still had on the rose-colored glasses that tinted our world view. I fully believed there could never be a problem so big that it would cause divorce for us; it was *impossible.*

Divorce was not an option; I made that vow with one crucial assumption: marriage would be a safe, healthy, and loving environment. I believed that commitment meant loyalty, tenderness, partnership, and love. What I didn't realize then was how easily that same promise could be twisted into a chain, something that would be used against me later, not to protect the marriage but to keep me trapped inside of it.

As our marriage began to unravel, I realized I had to confront my beliefs, my faith, and the very Scriptures that had been turned against me. I had not yet realized that my struggle was not with God; it was with the distortion that happens when His Word is twisted into a tool of control. In the hands of others, truth had become tangled, and so had I.

As the abuse grew more frequent, one verse became a constant weapon: *"Wives, submit to your husbands"* (Ephesians 5:22 NKJV). It was thrown at me like a command to stay quiet and obey. And somehow, I believed it. And that is where the words stopped. The rest of the passage, God's call for husbands to love with sacrifice and tenderness, was left unsaid, as if it did not exist. Just three verses later, Scripture says, *"Husbands, love your wives, just as Christ also loved the church and gave Himself for her"* (Ephesians 5:25 NKJV). The silence around that verse was deafening. It was as if only the words that could keep me small and controlled were worthy of being spoken, while those that demanded mutual love, sacrifice, and honor were erased.

Over the years, as I have shared my story and listened to others, I have discovered I am far from alone. Again and again, I have heard how *Ephesians 5:22 "Wives, submit to your husbands"* was wielded like a weapon against women in situations much like mine. For many survivors, it was not just their spouse who misused this verse. Family members, friends, even church leaders repeated it as though it were a command from God to stay silent and endure. Instead of offering protection, these voices reinforced the abuser's control, layering spiritual guilt on top of physical and emotional pain. What's tragic is that this kind of counsel does not simply keep a woman in harm's way, it wounds her soul all over again. It tells her that her suffering is somehow holy, that her silence is her duty, and that leaving would mean failing God. This kind of distortion does not reflect the heart of Christ; it revictimizes the already wounded and drives them deeper into isolation and despair.

Hearing this feedback again and again helped me realize something painful: so many survivors carry not only the bruises of abuse, but also the burden of distorted theology. Ephesians 5:22 is just one example. Other verses, too, are often used in ways that deepen wounds instead of bringing God's healing truth. Abusers twist verses on submission, forgiveness, and marriage into chains that bind rather than truths that set free.

My spiritual pain was compounded when a friend, who knew intimate details of the abuse, things I had just shared with her, began leaving large heart-shaped signs in our yard with Bible verses about the sanctity of marriage and how God hates divorce. The signs were clearly decorated by her young children. I remember standing in the yard, staring at those signs, asking myself: *How could she know what I went through and still do this?* Instead of love, those messages felt like judgment that was broadcast to the whole neighborhood, posted in my own front yard.

It was just a few short weeks later, after some threatening text messages, when I needed to ask the court to protect me and my children from my husband through an order of protection (OP). After I had the OP in hand, the court told me to make copies and share them with my kids' school, any organizations they were involved in, and our church. So that is exactly what I did. I started with the places where my children spent time without me, those felt the most urgent. Once I had dropped copies off at their school and extracurricular activity locations, I turned my attention to our church.

I will never forget walking into the church office. My eyes were still swollen from crying all morning during the OP application process. I explained to the church secretary, in the briefest way I could manage, what was happening. I told her about the OP and that my husband was legally prohibited from coming near me or our children. She accepted the copy and said she would pass it on to the pastor, who would follow up with me.

A few hours later, the phone rang. It was the secretary. She said the pastor had asked her to call me. Then she delivered a blow I did not see coming: the church would *not* honor my OP. They would not ask him to stay away, even though I was the one who was actively involved in the church, and he had no roles or responsibilities there.

She explained that if I still wanted to attend, I would have to make sure I arrived before he did each week. If I didn't, I needed to have a backup lined up to step in and handle the ministries I led. I had been running a Bible study for about 40 children, ages 8-10 every week, but now they were telling me I would need someone ready to lead that group if my husband showed up first. The church secretary finished the conversation with "We just can't take sides in this matter."

I was stunned. How could this be happening? I had given them clear proof, the OP included copies of the threatening text messages that had forced me to seek court protection. Yet they were treating it like a matter of choosing sides in a middle school argument.

As I hung up, it felt like the air left my lungs. I could barely breathe. In that moment, I knew I could never safely return to the church I had loved so deeply. By refusing to protect me and my children, they were asking me to play along with a dangerous game, one I would not risk. What began as my husband weaponizing the Bible had now grown into something larger: a pastor perpetuating harm under the guise of neutrality.

A few weeks later, a friend from church called and invited me to lunch. I was thrilled at the chance to see her. It was something normal, something kind, two emotions I hadn't felt in quite some time. The next day, we hugged tightly and started catching up. But then her expression grew serious. She told me that at church the previous week, my soon-to-be ex-husband had stood up during prayer time, and he asked the congregation to pray for both of us, telling them that I'd left him and that he was absolutely sure I must have found another man. She said he shared with the church that he couldn't think of another reason why I would have left him.

I blinked at her. "What?" I asked, stunned. She repeated what he said to everyone. I felt numb. How could this be? He knew exactly why we were divorcing. He knew why the court had granted the OP. Yet there he was, standing in front of the entire church, twisting the story and painting me as an adulteress. At that moment, I knew one thing for certain: I never wanted to date again, and marriage was absolutely out of the question.

Until that moment, almost no one from church had reached out to me, aside from two close friends. But after his announcement, my social media inbox started to fill with messages from church members I barely even knew. I ignored some of the messages at first. Then I started responding, telling them I had left because of abuse. I wanted to save my reputation. I wanted them to know I had not left my husband because of a nefarious affair. I had an OP in place. Once I shared a tiny picture of what life had been like for us, the messages changed: *"Pray harder." "Submit more." "Be patient; God will change him." "Don't give up on your marriage."* These words, usually spoken by people who thought they were offering spiritual wisdom, only added to the weight I was already carrying. Instead of comfort or encouragement, they became accusations, suggesting that if the abuse continued, it must be because I wasn't praying enough, submitting enough, or believing enough. Each phrase implied that the responsibility for saving the marriage rested entirely on my shoulders, while the abuser's sin and choices went unchallenged.

At first, I carried tremendous guilt, and the messages from my church members hit me hard. Those little seeds of doubt crept in during those silent moments I had to reflect: *Had I not prayed enough? Did*

I fail to submit enough? Had I been too impatient? And if nearly twenty years wasn't enough time, how much longer was I supposed to wait for God to change him? Those questions haunted me.

It took countless tears, hours of therapy, and the steady support of healthy friends, family, and a new church before I could even begin to unravel the lies I had absorbed. Slowly, I came to understand that prayer is not a magic formula that overrides someone else's choices. God doesn't force His will on anyone, each of us carries the gift and the responsibility of free will. No amount of my prayers was ever going to make my abuser change. Over time, I began to see how destructive those distorted messages had been, and just how much work it would take to untangle them from the truth of God's heart.

Have you ever believed God was asking you to stay in a place that was destroying you? Maybe you thought your endurance was proof of faith, or that your silence meant submission, or that suffering somehow proved your devotion. Maybe you convinced yourself that if you just prayed harder, loved deeper, and forgave quicker, God would bless your obedience. But the truth is, God never calls His children to remain in a place that crushes their spirit or strips away their dignity. That voice urging you to stay no matter the cost was not His, it was the voice of manipulation, twisting Scripture to hold you in a dangerous place.

I am a Christian. I believe in the sanctity of marriage. God designed marriage as a covenant of love, mutual respect, and spiritual unity. But we also serve a God who sees, hears, and cares deeply for those who suffer, especially at the hands of another. When marriage becomes a place of violence, fear, and control, God's heart breaks.

Jesus clearly upheld the sanctity of Marriage (Matthew 19:3-9). His ministry also centered on compassion and restoration. He confronted the legalistic thinking of the Pharisees when they valued rules above people. When marriage becomes a place of danger, a place of abuse, the covenant between a husband and wife has already been violated. The person who is seeking safety is not the one that broke their vow to love, honor, and protect.

Throughout the Bible we see how God shows Himself as the One that defends the oppressed. He commands His people to protect those that are mistreated (Psalm 82:3-4). God values the safety and dignity of His children above the preservation of an image of marriage that has already been corrupted by abuse. It is not ungodly to leave an abusive marriage. It is an act of courage and alignment with God's heart for justice. Just as God delivered Israel from the hand of Pharaoh, He desires to deliver His children from the bondage of fear and harm.

Marriage was intended to be lifelong, there's no doubt about that. But, in cases of abuse, divorce is not a rejection of God's ideal; it is a recognition that sin has destroyed the sacredness of the bond. God's grace meets us even in the ashes of broken vows. For those who have endured abuse, separation and divorce can be steps toward safety, healing, and restored faith.

When the fog of trauma begins to lift, hope gently enters in. Freedom, safety, and restoration are found in God's heart. He does not delight in your pain, He longs to see you wholly restored. Stepping away from what destroys you is not walking away from God's will. You are not outside of God's will for choosing safety.

God's plan for your life includes peace, dignity, and healing. He still has a purpose for you.

When faith has been twisted into a weapon, the process of reclaiming it doesn't happen overnight. It takes patience, courage, and a willingness to face both pain and truth. It unfolds as we lean into God's love, reclaim our voices, and rediscover who we are in Christ. For me, untangling the knots of faith was like carefully working through a rope pulled tight for years: slow, deliberate, and sometimes frustrating, but absolutely necessary for freedom.

These next steps are not rules to follow, but guideposts that helped me move from surviving to truly living.

Step 1: Therapy and Wise Counsel

One of the first lifelines I found was safe, trauma-informed counseling. I was so afraid of going to counseling. I didn't know what to expect, I had never been to a therapist before. I made an appointment with a therapist that participated with my insurance. I prayed she would be a good fit. I had convinced myself that this woman would give me the same message I had heard from so many outside influences: I hadn't done enough.

Her waiting room was warm and inviting, starkly different from the very corporate building her office was in. The floor was dark wood with several stylish yet comfy chairs lining the walls. It wasn't long before she came through the side door and greeted me by name. She was a tiny woman, much shorter than my 5'4" height. I followed her down the short hallway to her office. She sat in an overstuffed chair and invited me to sit on the loveseat. She had her pad and pen lying on her lap and a warm smile on her face. She put me at ease immediately.

She was insightful and soft-spoken, a combination that eased my soul and spoke to my heart. She was a Christian woman and, although we were different faiths, she understood the lens in which I had viewed marriage for all those years. She helped me name what had really happened: it was abuse. This was the first time I was really ready to own that label. She reminded me that what I endured was not God's design for marriage. Therapy gave me tools to recognize the lies I had internalized and to begin replacing them with truth.

Alongside therapy, wise counsel from trusted, spiritually mature and wise friends created a space where I could process without judgment. These voices reminded me that God is not the author of confusion or abuse, but the giver of peace and safety. The shift in my mindset was not immediate, it took time. And healing wasn't linear, sometimes it felt like I would take one step forward and two steps back. But I was determined to push forward and do the work to create a healthy environment for my children.

Step 2: Returning to Scripture in Context

Part of untangling my faith meant learning to approach the Bible with fresh eyes. This was really tough. I had not picked up my Bible other than to use it at church in many years. I had lost that personal relationship with Him because I was angry with Him for not changing my situation. For so long, I had only heard certain verses quoted to me, verses meant to control or silence. I knew there was more to those verses, but I didn't dare point that out. When I finally opened the Bible and read passages in their entirety, a very different picture emerged. Ephesians 5, for example, does not stop at *"Wives, submit to your husbands"*; it calls husbands to love their wives *"just as Christ also loved the church and gave Himself for her."* That is a picture of sacrificial love, not domination.

As I continued to study, my view of God and his character started to shift. I began to notice how consistently Scripture reveals God's heart for the vulnerable: *"The Lord is near to the brokenhearted"* (Psalm 34:18) *"He has sent me to heal the brokenhearted, to proclaim liberty to the captives"* (Isaiah 61:1) "He heals the brokenhearted and binds up their wounds" (Psalm 147:3). These verses became anchors of truth, reminding me that Jesus's ministry was always about setting people free in Him, not keeping them trapped in relationships that break their body or mind.

The Bible so clearly teaches us about God's character, but for many of us, those truths were once clouded by the distorted messages we had been taught. We read in John 3:17 *"For God did not send His Son into the world to condemn the world, but that the world through Him might be saved."* When we return to Scripture with new eyes, we begin to see that God does not control or condemn, He is a God of compassion, justice, and freedom. We realize the difference between what was imposed on us through manipulation and what is actually revealed about God's heart. Reading the Bible in this way allows us to separate truth from distortion, healing from harm, and love from fear. It becomes less about rules to keep us bound and more about our relationship with a God who desires to see us flourishing. This shift is not just intellectual, it's deeply personal, reshaping how we see God, ourselves, and the life of freedom we are invited to live.

And yet, even with fresh eyes, faith is not restored in a single moment. It takes wrestling, studying, questioning, and pouring out the rawest parts of our hearts before God. That's where honest prayer becomes the next step, learning to bring our unfiltered grief, anger, and hope into His presence, and discovering He can handle it all.

Step 3: Honest Prayer

I had been angry at God for quite some time, years, in fact. While I was still married, I would get in the shower every morning, put my face in the spray of hot water and let the tears flow down my face. While I cried in the shower, I sent up silent prayers, questioning God and asking for answers: *Why aren't You changing my husband? Why are You allowing me to be hurt this way? Where are You God?* I still had a very strong faith, and I knew God was watching over me, but why wasn't He changing my circumstances?

After escaping I knew that I needed to have some tough conversations with God. I felt the need for Him now more than ever, but I also needed to understand Him in a way that I never had. Before the abuse I had a strong prayer life, talking with God throughout the day. During my marriage my prayers were offered up in anguish, and I became silent throughout the day. But after escaping my prayer life was beginning to look very different. My prayers went up without ceasing, they were even more raw and unfiltered but now they also included praise and thanks. But many times, my prayers allowed me to pour out my anger, grief, and confusion honestly before Him. Sometimes I didn't have the words, only tears that flowed. And instead of condemnation, I found a God who listened with compassion. In those honest moments, I began to rediscover who God really is. He is not a taskmaster demanding my silence, but a Father who holds space for my pain and invites me to bring every part of my story to Him.

During this time of very honest prayer, I was reading the book of Psalms. This book is raw, unfiltered, and profoundly human. David poured out his heart in every possible emotion: the joy, the sorrow, the anger, the confusion, and even the moments of despair that felt too heavy to bear. He didn't hide his doubts or fears, nor did he pretend that life was perfect. I identified so much with the words David wrote. I realized that it was okay to bring my whole self to God: the good, the bad, and the ugly. Psalms taught me that honest expression before God is not a lack of faith, but a deep, trusting relationship with my Father and truest friend. He listens, comforts, and restores. It became a model for the kind of prayer I needed: one where I could speak truthfully, without fear of judgment or condemnation. Some days, when I had no words, I prayed through the Psalms, using David's words in place of my own.

God was so merciful with me. He was gracious enough to show me whose I am. I am His. I belong to Him. He is my Father, and I am His daughter. What a beautiful God! In the midst of confusion, fear, and heartache, He reminded me that my identity is not defined by the abuse I endured, the lies I was told, or the expectations of others. My worth is anchored in Him alone, unshaken by circumstances. He met me in my brokenness, holding me gently, teaching me that I am loved not for what I do or how long I endure, but simply for who I am, His child. That truth was an eye-opener, it became a foundation to rebuild from, a constant reminder that no matter how tangled my faith had become, His love was steady, unchanging, and fiercely protective. It's a love that heals, restores, and finally sets the captive heart free.

****

Faith after abuse doesn't look like blind obedience, it looks like healing and discernment that leads to true freedom. For years, I thought faith meant keeping quiet, submitting my free will, and sacrificing myself to keep peace at any cost. But real faith, the kind deeply rooted in God's true character, doesn't demand silence in the face of harm. It calls us to bring light to the atrocities committed. It calls us to speak truth so healing can begin.

The Bible does not show us a Father that is steeped in chaos and confusion. Nowhere in the Bible do we read that God encourages or even condones abusing the people you are supposed to love and cherish. As I have come to know God and His character, I've come to know He is a God of order, He is not a tyrant who demands unquestioning loyalty to a destructive relationship. He is the One who lifts burdens, not the one who adds to them. He is the One who hears the cry of the oppressed, who binds up wounds, and who steps into broken places to restore what has been shattered.

Truly understanding faith after abuse has meant a paradigm shift, I've had to learn what trust in God really looks like. It is no longer about letting others dictate what I should believe or how I should live. It is about discernment, testing every message I hear against the truth of Scripture and the character of God. It is about healing, allowing space for my heart to mend without shame or the pressure of outside distorted Biblical views. It is about knowing that God's love never cages me in but always leads me to salvation and freedom in Jesus Christ. You are not "less" because your marriage ended; you are loved, seen, and treasured by the One who redeems.

Faith untangled is faith reclaimed, no longer bound by manipulation, but anchored in truth and love. It is a faith that stands firm, not in fear of punishment, but in confidence of God's goodness. And it is a faith that points forward, reminding me that what was once twisted can be made clear again in the hands of our redeeming God.

Chapter Gate Reminder:
The following chapter continues anonymized, paraphrased recollections intended to protect privacy.

Chapter 6: Paper Chains

What happens when leaving an abuser doesn't end the abuse? What if the courtroom, the very place that's supposed to provide safety and fairness, becomes another weapon in your abuser's hands? For many survivors, the abuse doesn't stop when the relationship ends. Instead, it shifts into a new method, a new battleground where legal papers replace threats, and court hearings become another form of intimidation. This pattern is often called legal abuse. The amount of paperwork generated by someone using the legal system as another form of abuse is overwhelming. These documents create paper chains that seem to endlessly tie a survivor to their abuser.

The first time I really understood about the legal system being used as another tool of control was when a motion was filed against me alleging that I wasn't allowing the children to have contact with their father, even though there was an active order of protection in place. He wasn't legally allowed to be physically near them, however, the OP allowed him to call them and text them a few times during the week. I remember feeling so confused. He had not called or texted in months. My children had their own cell phones, and our cell phone records clearly showed that no numbers were blocked on their phones. Not only were phone numbers not blocked, but the records showed that only a few text messages were sent to my daughter over many months, and none were sent to my son. And yet here I was, standing in court, having to prove that I wasn't keeping him from having these calls and texts with his children.

This wasn't the first motion filed against me that didn't make any sense to me. But, in this motion, there was a request that the judge take away my driver's license as punishment for keeping him from the children. I was stunned. The judge ruled in my favor on this case, but that didn't stop more motions from being filed.

Legal abuse happens when an abuser uses the court system in an attempt to maintain control after separation and divorce. Instead of physical or emotional tactics, they misuse legal processes to intimidate, exhaust, or financially strain the survivor. This can look like filing unnecessary motions, dragging out proceedings, or making false claims, all with the goal of creating confusion and pressure. It is emotionally draining and designed to make you feel powerless while pretending to follow the letter of the law.

It often begins with small, seemingly ordinary actions: a missed deadline, repeated continuances, a sudden motion in court for an outrageous accusation. Each one feels manageable in isolation, but together they create a storm that can leave even the strongest person questioning their ability to fight, to survive, to protect themselves and their children.

I want to be very clear, legal abuse is real. It is intentional. And it is devastating. It preys on fear, confusion, and exhaustion, and it thrives in the gray areas of the law where the rules seem to favor whoever has more resources, more time, or more persistence.

I share just a few of my own experiences, not to dwell on the pain, but to shine a light on the tactics, the warning signs, and the strategies that can help you protect yourself, or someone you love. Being the recipient of legal abuse is not a reflection of a person's strength, intelligence, or worth, it is a tactic used to control, and it can be confronted with knowledge and the right legal support, family solidarity, and the care of a healthy faith community.

****

Early one morning, I worked up the courage to share with my husband that I was going to meet with a divorce attorney later that day. I didn't know what his reaction would be. I half expected a fight, or at least a flash of anger. Instead, he looked at me calmly and said it was time to file the paperwork. His indifference caught me off guard. We had been living separate lives under the same roof for a long time. The in-house separation was not improving our marriage, things definitely were not getting any better. In some ways, they were even worse than before.

Because he seemed agreeable that morning, I let myself believe the process might be civil, maybe even peaceful. We had already talked about how we would divide the house proceeds, the furniture, and all the "stuff" that had once represented a shared life. He'd written everything we agreed to down on a master list, neatly organized, and handed me a copy before I left for the lawyer's office. It felt strangely transactional, like we were closing a business rather than ending a marriage.

Later that afternoon, I walked into Charlie's office, which I later realized was the start of my legal journey. He was young, fresh out of law school, and far less expensive than the other lawyers I had considered. I assumed that his inexperience was the reason that his hourly price was lower than the other lawyer's fees I was quoted. But, even with his inexperience, there was something steady about him. He listened more than he spoke, and he knew how to ask questions in a way that put me at ease. I needed to calm more than confidence or courtroom bravado. I wasn't looking for a fighter. I was looking for someone who knew the law well and could help me navigate what felt like the unraveling of my entire life.

When I handed Charlie the list my husband had written, I told him we had already agreed on how to split our belongings. Charlie glanced at the paper and nodded with quiet professionalism. He said he would include the division of property into our Marriage Dissolution Agreement. I remember feeling a strange mix of relief and disbelief, as if the simple act of writing down who got what could somehow untangle years of pain.

That phrase stuck with me, *Marriage Dissolution.* It sounded so sterile, so cold, yet that's exactly what divorce is: the legal unraveling of the vows we made, the official ending of unfulfilled dreams and broken hearts. But at least this process would be amicable for us. Or so I thought.

When I returned to the house later that day, my husband told me he had sat outside the courthouse all day until they locked the doors in the late afternoon. The purpose of sitting there was to stop me from meeting with my lawyer. I didn't know why he would try to stop me since only that morning he had agreed this was what needed to happen. I remember him sharing something about a divorce would only put us into financial ruin, so we should stay together for financial reasons.

I didn't acknowledge that reasoning, I simply told him that my lawyer's office wasn't in the courthouse. At first, he looked surprised, then I felt the shift in the mood. It felt like there was anger bubbling just beneath the surface. He was under the mistaken impression that all lawyers offices were located inside the courthouse. That's when I knew something had changed. It wasn't long before the legal system, something which I had believed would simply finalize an agreement, suddenly became another battlefield to stand on.

Understanding Legal Abuse

Legal abuse is one of the most hidden, least understood forms of post-separation and post-divorce control. So many people assume that once someone leaves an abusive relationship, the worst is over. But for countless survivors, the abuse simply shifts into a new form: manipulation through the court system.

Abusers know that court is a place with rules, deadlines, and procedures that can be confusing and intimidating. They also know these systems cost money, time, and emotional energy. By exploiting the legal process, they create a constant state of stress and uncertainty for the survivor. The post-separation abuse typically no longer looks like shouting, hitting, or controlling. Instead, it shows up as stacks of paperwork, endless hearings, false accusations, and threats hidden inside legal documents.

Some of the most common tactics include:

- **Dragging out divorce or custody cases**: this prevents closure, causes added stress and fear, and often prevents someone from moving on with their life in a healthy way.

- **Filing unnecessary or repetitive motions**: this depletes finances and drains energy. It can also be used to inflict fear and intimidation when requests for punishment (e.g. taking away a driver's license) are included in the motions.

- **Using custody disputes as a weapon**: demanding changes to newly court-ordered agreements simply to destabilize the survivor or children.

- **Making false accusations**: forcing the survivor to defend themselves and risking rulings against a survivor based on lies.

- **Deliberately missing deadlines**: requesting continuances or filing in the wrong jurisdiction to cause costly delays.

- **Insisting on in-person hearings**: unreasonable demands are used to force unwanted contact to further intimidate a survivor.

- **Smearing the survivor's reputation**: sometimes this looks like insinuations that a survivor is unfit, unstable, or has been unfaithful. But sometimes these are blatant statements made against a survivor to try to convince others of the lies being told.

The legal process often felt like a roller coaster ride in the dark. There were so many unpredictable twists and turns. After trying to stop me from going into the lawyer's office to file the divorce paperwork, he again shared that he was agreeable with the divorce, with one caveat. He shared that he would sign the papers if I watched a faith-based movie with him that talked about a couple who came back from the brink of divorce. At first, I resisted it. It felt humiliating to be held hostage by such a condition. But after weeks of delay, I finally agreed, just to move the process forward. The movie wasn't even about abuse. It had nothing to do with my reasons for leaving. And yet, he used it as leverage to keep control.

A few days after we watched the movie, he showed up at my lawyer's office to sign the papers. But after seeing my attorney for the first time, he became angry and started throwing verbal accusations, suggesting I was romantically involved with my lawyer simply because my husband thought my lawyer was young and attractive. He left my lawyer's office without signing the Dissolution of Marriage Agreement. That's when I finally accepted that my divorce had almost no chance of being amicable. It was going to be contested, messy, emotionally draining, and costly.

The legal abuse didn't stop when the divorce proceedings concluded, it continued for years, until our youngest child turned 18. It looked like repeated, baseless motions that had no legal merit. These motions drained not only time, but also my bank account and my energy. Frivolous filings can force survivors to take time off work, pay more legal fees, and relive painful experiences in front of a judge, even when the outcome is predictable. Over the next several years, I lived this reality. Because of his repeated dangerous behaviors, the court put multiple orders of protection in place for me and the kids. Even with those protections, he kept dragging me back into court. He filed multiple motions, asking for reduced child support, demanding that I pay him for various things even though the children were with me 100% of the time. He was pushing to end child support for our youngest early in his senior year of high school and long before our son turned eighteen. All of this while he hadn't seen the children in several years. That is the nature of legal abuse: it isn't about fairness or justice, it's about control. Survivors often describe it as feeling like they are still chained to their abuser, long after leaving the relationship, wondering when it will end. After years of responding to these motions, I often wondered if I would ever be truly free.

Practical Strategies for Survivors

Survivors can't stop an abuser from misusing the legal system, but there are ways to limit the damage and reclaim your life. As of the writing of this book, only eight states have specific laws on the books that directly address legal abuse, or litigation abuse. The states that do not have specific laws about legal abuse include coercive control as a form of abuse that is legally recognized. Some states include legal abuse under the category of coercive control. However, in my case, even with the continual motions filed it would have been more costly for me to address the issue of legal abuse and go to trial, than to deal with the motions being filed against me. This is what keeps a survivor feeling trapped.

Here are a few practical strategies that can help to ease the pain of legal abuse:

1. Document Everything

One of the most important tools you can have is solid documentation. I saved everything: motions, emails, texts, voicemails. I kept them both digitally and in print. My print copies went into binders so I could quickly find what I needed under colorful tabs: Marital Dissolution Agreement, Parenting Plan, Threats and Accusations, Fraud, Medical Expenses, Phone Records, Motions, Court Rulings, and Orders of Protection (just to name a few). I also kept a timeline of upcoming court dates and put reminders in my online calendar. I kept notes on what documentation I would need to respond to each new motion. As I discovered documentation that was needed, I would add a little sticky flag to the document so I could find it easily later.

Each time I went to court, I carried the most up-to-date binder with me. More than once, those records made all the difference. They proved that my name and social security number had been used to open a credit card in another state with over $1,200 in charges. They provided evidence that I hadn't received any child support, even though it was court-ordered, which ultimately led to garnished wages. They showed the judge that no phone numbers were ever blocked on my children's phones. My binder gave me the proof I needed to expose false claims. Keeping careful records helped turn the chaos into something manageable, something survivable.

2. Limit Direct Communication

During divorce proceedings, courts often require mediation when there are disagreements about how to divide assets or arrange parenting time. If you are asked to attend mediation, it's essential to request a separate conference room for you and your lawyer. The mediator will move between the rooms to relay proposals, acceptances, and counteroffers. This approach keeps you from sitting face-to-face with an abuser who may try to intimidate you, making the process much safer and less stressful. My lawyer, Charlie, highly recommended separate conference rooms for my mediation, and it was a lifesaver. He worked it out that I didn't even have to see my ex-husband since there was an active order of protection at that time. The court would have allowed us to be in the same room for mediation, even with the OP, but Charlie knew how stressful it would be for me to have to be face-to-face with him all day in a conference room.

Much of the communication with my ex-husband had to be done through our lawyers because of active orders of protection. There were still times when we needed to communicate about things: the children's health, the sale of the house, changing vehicle titles, etc. During the short windows of time when the order of protection was no longer in place, I would receive texts with veiled threats that would send me into a panic.

When children are involved, using court-approved parenting communication apps can take a lot of the tension out of high-conflict situations. I didn't learn about these apps until my son was almost 18. These apps are typically set up to send copies of all messages to both lawyers. Some apps have filters that help prevent threats. If buying the app is not financially feasible, another way to limit direct contact is to have all communication go through your lawyer's office. If you must communicate, keep messages short, factual, and neutral. Stick to the information that is necessary.

3. Work With Trauma-Informed Legal Professionals

Seek a lawyer who understands domestic abuse dynamics, not just family law. Ask potential lawyers how they handle high-conflict cases or abusive ex-partners. In many abuse cases, there has never been a police report filed, or charges brought prior to divorce filings. It is important to ask if they have experience with cases where no legal documentation of abuse exists. If finances are a concern, explore legal aid, domestic violence advocacy centers, or pro bono programs, as there are often options for survivors.

My lawyer, Charlie, was brand new and had never handled a high-conflict case like mine. However, even as a new lawyer, he had zero tolerance for toxic or abusive behavior. Charlie and I learned together how to navigate these difficult situations. He would request small but crucial accommodations, such as giving me ten minutes to exit the courthouse so I could make it safely to my car. He was always willing to have his office handle communication between me and my ex-husband through the opposing lawyer, helping me maintain boundaries and protect myself. Having a lawyer who worked to understand the dynamics of abuse made all the difference, turning what could have broken me into a process that was manageable.

4. Set Boundaries

You have every right to set boundaries, both around court appearances and your life. For court appearances, ask your lawyer to arrange a room where you can wait privately before hearings. If the court is unable to accommodate your request, work with your lawyer to have designated areas in the courthouse where you will wait with your lawyer and where your spouse/ex-spouse will wait with their lawyer where you cannot see each other. Request remote appearances, if allowed. Bring a trusted support person to sit with you, even if they are only in court for moral support. Place someone between you and your ex-spouse while inside the courtroom, so the line-of-site is broken. This prevents someone looking on with threatening looks or scowls.

Setting boundaries in your personal life, in many cases, means asking the court for protection through an Order of Protection, Restraining Order, or Protection from Abuse Order (names vary depending on the state). I know how scary this can be. I've been there, done that, and got the button. I can't tell you how many times I've heard that an order of protection is "just a piece of paper." Many people don't feel that the OP does anything to protect them. And while the OP is *technically* just a piece of paper, that piece of paper gives law enforcement the ability to protect you in a more effective way. That piece of paper allows an officer to protect you (and where applicable, your children) no matter where you are. That protection from that piece of paper doesn't only apply to your home, but extends to school, work, church, and anywhere else you frequent. The OP creates a legal boundary that allows law enforcement to protect you, when they wouldn't otherwise be able to.

I know how scary it is to just fill out the request for the emergency order of protection. The questions that swirl through your mind can be paralyzing. *How will they react? Will they escalate? Will they come after me once they find out? What if the judge denies the request? How do I stay safe while waiting for it to be served? How do I tell the kids? Who do I call if the order is violated? Is he allowed to contact me through friends and family?* These questions, and many more like them, are all valid concerns.

How will they react? Will they escalate? Will they come after me once they find out? No one ever fully knows the answer to these questions in advance. That's why it is so important to have a safety plan in place. I also cannot stress enough how important it is to go to a shelter during that time period while you are waiting for the court hearing to happen after getting a temporary or emergency order of protection. This time period is statistically very dangerous for a woman. The safety plan is the safety net that can mean the difference between life and death.

What if the judge denies the request? Even if the judge denies the request, it doesn't mean your story isn't valid, or that help isn't available. Sometimes judges need more information, or the law requires specific evidence before issuing the order. You can refile. Reach out to an advocate and ask for help. This moment doesn't define your worth or your safety plan, it's simply one step in the process. At the end of this book there are resources that can help you to find an advocate in the United States.

How do I stay safe while waiting for it to be served? Please, please go to a shelter. I know it's uncomfortable, scary, and unknown. But going to a shelter will help to keep you safe from your abuser. When survivors stay with friends or family, it puts the survivor and their hosts at risk. There are so many facets of the safety plan that apply here: Staying at a shelter, getting a burner phone, having the car scanned for trackers, making sure all of the children's devices have location services turned off or are completely left behind. The safety plan is crucial during this time.

How do I tell the kids? Sigh. This part is never easy. Explaining to your children that an order of protection is in place against their father can be heartbreaking. For me, it was one of the hardest conversations I've ever had. Because of the nature of the threats, I couldn't even tell my children why I had to file that first order. They were simply too young to understand.

What helped me a lot was praying before I spoke to them, asking God to give me the right words at the right time. The best advice I can offer is to be as honest and open as possible, in a way that suits their age and emotional understanding. Remember, you're not alone in this conversation, the Lord can guide you, bringing peace where fear once lived.

Who do I call if the order is violated? No ifs, ands, or buts you absolutely call **911 immediately.** Every. Single. Time.

When my order of protection was violated, I hesitated. Fear and uncertainty kept me from picking up the phone right away. It took me a couple days to report it, and looking back, I wish I had called the moment it happened. The violation wasn't violent, he didn't hit me or physically threaten me that day. He approached me while I was in my car and started talking about his "rights" with the kids, even though the order clearly said otherwise. I told myself it wasn't serious enough to call, but the truth is, **any** violation matters. And when I finally reported it, law enforcement said that it was serious. The officer explained that abusers often "test the waters" with non-violent violations of an order of protection before escalating to more serious ones. He also emphasized how important it is to report **every** violation, no matter how small it may seem. If those early, non-violent incidents go unreported, a survivor may later be questioned as to why no action was taken when the abuser previously violated the order without consequence. Reporting each violation helps establish a clear pattern of behavior and strengthens your protection moving forward.

I understand how easy it is to second-guess yourself or worry about how law enforcement will respond. But please remember this: your safety comes first. You are not overreacting. You are not a burden. You are standing in the protection God has already made available to you. Don't let fear silence you. You have the right to be safe, and you have the right to be heard.

Is he allowed to contact me through friends and family? Each OP will have different stipulations. My order of protection did not allow for him to contact me through friends or family. Although, he did contact me through friends and family. I didn't report those violations because the people that relayed messages "didn't want to get involved," so I didn't have any witnesses that would stand up for me. They didn't want to give a statement to the police or testify in a courtroom. I could have asked my lawyer to subpoena them, but they would have been considered a hostile witness. I didn't want that. However, if I had it to do over again, I would have reported it. I would have told the police about these messages being relayed to me, even if that report didn't result in an official violation of the order. It is so important to keep an official paper trail of all violations.

5. Expect Financial Drain

Legal battles can quickly become financially exhausting, so it's important to plan ahead. Budget for ongoing legal costs as realistically as possible and keep a detailed written record of any excessive or frivolous filings. These records can help you request reimbursement or further action from the court later.

Whenever possible, use the resources available to you. There are free resources available that do not have income threshold requirements. If your income is such that you are unable to afford a lawyer, seek out free or low-cost legal aid organizations, survivor advocacy programs, or church-based support groups that can help lighten the financial and emotional load. If your situation qualifies, ask the court for reimbursement of lawyer's fees if permitted by law.

To manage legal costs, try grouping your questions and sending them in one email to your lawyer's paralegal instead of making multiple calls to your lawyer. Paralegals usually bill at a lower hourly rate, which helps preserve your retainer funds and keeps your case moving forward efficiently.

6. Prioritize Emotional and Spiritual Support

The court process can make you feel small, unheard, and oftentimes invisible. Surround yourself with people who remind you that you are loved, valued, and seen. Join support groups for survivors. Lean on your faith community, remembering that God sees the truth, even when systems are slow to recognize it.

At the time of my divorce there were limited resources where I lived for domestic abuse survivors. I looked to find support groups, but nothing was available. Today there are organizations like The Family Justice Center (FJC) that operate in many states across the United States. The FJC offers multiple services under one roof to abuse survivors. Some of the services offered to survivors are: Legal Aide, free counseling, music therapy, outdoor therapy, and seminars.

7. Stay Focused on the End Goal

Legal abuse is meant to wear you down. Recognize the tactic and refuse to let every filing or delay steal your peace. Remember that the courtroom, and the one filing the motions, doesn't define your identity. You are more than the accusations, more than the mountains of paperwork, more than the court appearances. Celebrate small wins: a motion dismissed, a ruling in your favor, a boundary upheld, a day when you held your ground. These small victories should be prayed about and recorded in a journal, so on the days you are discouraged you can look back and see how God took care of you in the past.

****

Finding yourself trapped in a battle of control, manipulation, and intimidation is heavy, tedious, exhausting, and scary at times. Just when safety and peace seem to be in sight, the process continues in the courts. Remember that all these games an abuser plays are not the final word. By documenting carefully, setting boundaries, seeking the right legal support, and leaning on trusted friends, family, and faith, survivors can reclaim a sense of autonomy and freedom.

Over time, the constant filings, delays, and false accusations will lose some of their power. The paper chains of endless paperwork will eventually break. You will still get tired, and that's ok. Take time for yourself, time to rest. The lesson that remains is that you are strong and capable. You can endure, persevere, and navigate even the most frustrating and intimidating situations with the tools you have. Even when it feels like the rules, paperwork, and people involved are stacked against you, you are capable of holding your ground and protecting your peace.

I may not personally know you or the specific challenges you are facing, but I am praying for you every day. I pray that you can see the glimmers of hope even when the situation seems hopeless. I pray that you will remember your worth, your resilience, and the truth that abuse is never a reflection of your value.

Step by step, moment by moment, you can reclaim your life, your voice, and your freedom. And even in the midst of legal battles, paperwork, and what feels like endless motions, God sees you, He knows your struggle, and He walks with you through it all. Hold on to hope, it is your anchor when everything else feels uncertain.

Chapter Gate Reminder:
The following chapter continues anonymized, paraphrased recollections intended to protect privacy.

Chapter 7: Who are you and why are you here?

The last few chapters were heavy. If you've been reading this book without a break, pause for a moment and take a few deep breaths. Let the weight of the stories, the warnings, and the realizations settle. It is very important to process what you've read.

Let's take a moment now for a simple prayer before we move on:

"Lord, I ask You to quiet my mind and calm my heart. Help me to hear Your voice above the noise of life, to see myself as Your daughter, and to understand the purpose You have placed within me. Guide me as I reflect on who you say I am and why You created me. Amen."

****

Many years ago, I worked for a man named Bob. He was the CEO and part owner of a company with nine locations across three different countries. He traveled on the corporate jet, lived in a beautiful home, and drove a top-of-the-line SUV. By most standards, he was quite comfortable. But what made Bob remarkable wasn't his wealth, it was that he knew who he was and Whose he was. Bob was a Christian man who openly shared his faith in company meetings, starting with prayer and reflecting on what Christ had done for him and the company.

At the time, the company had just purchased its ninth location. Meetings were scheduled with the new organization's leadership team to discuss how we would integrate that location into the rest of the company. At the start of the very first integration meeting, Bob shared a story that has stayed with me all these years.

Here's a summary of what he shared:

One evening, a Rabbi was returning home, deep in thought, when he inadvertently wandered into a Roman military outpost. A guard atop the fortress wall spotted him and called down, demanding, "Who are you, and why are you here?" Startled, the Rabbi asked the guard to repeat the question. Again, the guard said, "Who are you, and why are you here?" The Rabbi paused, then asked, "How much are you paid to ask that question?" The guard, taken aback, replied, "Two drachmas a week." The Rabbi then offered to pay the guard double if he would come to his house every morning and ask those same two questions: "Who are you?" and "Why are you here?"

These are questions for us to wrestle with every single day - Who are you and why are you here? The Rabbi turned a moment of confrontation into an invitation for self-reflection, and we are invited to do the same. As we explore our identity in Christ, these questions help us to reflect and have a deeper understanding of who we are, Whose we are, and the purpose God has uniquely designed for each of us.

I want you to pause with me here for a moment. How often do we feel lost in life, wondering who we are or what our purpose is? What if, just like the Rabbi, those moments of uncertainty are not mistakes, but invitations to discover ourselves more deeply in Christ? I want to explore these questions with you. Who are you? Why are you here? And how can the twists and turns of life guide you toward the answers you've been searching for?

When I first heard this story, I felt completely lost, I didn't know who I was, and I certainly didn't know why I was here. At that time, my identity and purpose seemed to exist only in being a mom to my two beautiful children. I have always loved being their mom; it was what got me out of bed each morning and put a smile on my face. But my identity in Christ was buried under a layer of lies and distorted interpretations of Scripture, convincing me that I was worthless in God's eyes.

After the separation and the divorce, I still saw myself through a lens that made me feel worthless, powerless, and without purpose. I knew I needed to find some sense of direction, for my kids' sake, but I wasn't even thinking that God could restore me, let alone use me for His purpose. My spirit felt broken, and my heart carried this heavy ache, like I could never be enough.

The work of healing and rediscovery was not easy.

It was my therapist who helped me to shift my perspective. She helped me see that my identity and my purpose were not tied to my ex-husband, and that a failed marriage didn't mean God had thrown me away. Through faith-based counseling, she helped me to lay a solid foundation, to start rebuilding my life, and to reclaim my voice. Slowly, gently, I began to understand that even in the midst of pain, God was still at work, shaping me, teaching me, and preparing me for the purpose He had always intended for me.

I had to face my past head-on, confront my brokenness, and dismantle the mask of perfection I had worn for so long. That mask had hidden my vulnerabilities, my fears, and my insecurities, but it was also suffocating my growth. I eventually began peeling back the mask and tearing down the walls I had so easily constructed so I could maintain an image of perfection. I started to see myself more clearly, not through the lens of shame or failure, but through God's eyes. I am a daughter of the King.

I also had to learn to be vulnerable. Admitting my weaknesses and asking for help was extremely difficult. How could I trust anyone else and allow them to see the real, broken me when I no longer even trusted myself? I have always been self-reliant, out of need. I can say I was proud even, and asking for help felt like failure. But each step of honesty brought freedom. Being authentic didn't make me weak; it made me whole. Slowly, I began to reclaim the pieces of myself I had hidden or ignored, and in doing so, I began to understand God's purpose for me.

As I began my journey to vulnerability, I started to see myself in a different light. Where I had previously looked at myself through the lens of failure and shame, I began to now see strength and courage. It wasn't an overnight change; it was a slow, sometimes painful process of peeling back layers of lies I had believed for years. I journaled my fears, prayed over my insecurities, and reminded myself daily of what Scripture says about who I am in Christ. I began to realize that my worth didn't come from perfection, accomplishments, or the approval of others, it came from God, and that truth started to reshape the way I saw myself.

Small Steps Matter

Even as I started to understand my identity, God revealed His calling to me in small, almost imperceptible ways. I didn't receive a single dramatic vision of what my life's work should be. Instead, He began with gentle nudges.

- A conversation with a friend who was struggling, where I shared a piece of my story and realized how much hope it could give someone else.

- Sitting with someone in grief and listening with patience, realizing my empathy could be a tool for God's work.

- Helping a neighbor with a small task, only to discover the joy of service multiplies when it is given in love.

Each of these small acts, seemingly ordinary, was a seed planted by God, preparing me for a larger calling. Slowly, my identity in Christ began to emerge from the shadows of doubt and fear. I realized that I wasn't only a mom, a worker, or a survivor. I am God's daughter, uniquely created and deeply loved, called to live for His glory. That revelation didn't erase the pain of my past, but it gave it new meaning. Every broken piece, every hardship, became part of the journey God was using to prepare me for the purpose He had planned all along. And with that understanding came a quiet confidence that no matter what twists and turns life would take, I was not lost. I was exactly where I needed to be, in His hands.

Friend, maybe you've been where I was, living with a polished version of yourself on the outside, while carrying a much different story inside. Maybe you've believed lies about your worth, or maybe you've carried guilt and shame for so long that it feels like part of who you are. If that's you, I want to remind you: you are not alone, and you don't have to stay there.

The truth is, God never called us to perfection, He called us to relationship with Him. He doesn't ask us to pretend or hide behind masks. Instead, He invites us to come to Him as we are: broken, messy, unsure, and in need of His love. And when we do, He begins the work of reshaping us, just like clay in the hands of the Potter (Isaiah 64:8).

Creating Beauty from Brokenness

The Japanese have an art form called kintsugi, which means "golden joinery." When a piece of pottery is broken, instead of throwing it away, an artist carefully repairs it with a special lacquer and mixes it with powdered gold. The cracks don't disappear, in fact, they become the most visible part of the piece. Instead of being signs of shame or weakness, the gold-filled fractures tell a story of restoration. The pottery is not only made whole again, but it becomes even more beautiful and more valuable because of its brokenness.

That's exactly what God does with us. As the master potter He doesn't discard us when life leaves us cracked and shattered. He takes every broken piece, the mistakes, the pain, the loss, and with His grace and love, He makes something new. Our scars don't have to be hidden; they can become the testimony of His healing power. Just like kintsugi pottery, our restored lives can shine even brighter because of the brokenness we've been through. Your cracks don't disqualify you; they are where God's golden grace shines through.

I look back now and realize that the very places I once felt most ashamed of (my divorce, my insecurities, my broken identity) are the very places where God poured His *golden grace*. Those cracks became part of my story, and instead of disqualifying me, they revealed the beauty of God's restoring work.

Even as I wrestled with the broken pieces of my life, God kept whispering His truth over me: "You are chosen." God's presence in my life was my biggest comfort, because for so long I believed I was discarded, unwanted, and left behind. But the truth of Scripture says something very different. Paul writes in Ephesians 1:4 (NKJV), "Just as He chose us in Him before the foundation of the world, that we should be holy and without blame before Him in love." Think about that for a moment, you and I were chosen by God before the world even began. Long before our mistakes, long before our heartbreak, even before we drew our first breath, God had already set His love on us.

Vulnerability as a Gateway to Purpose

And it's not just being chosen in some distant, impersonal way. Scripture reminds us that God calls us His own. In Isaiah 43:1 (NKJV), God says, "Fear not, for I have redeemed you; I have called you by your name; you are Mine." Those words undo the lies that tell us we're not enough. They remind us that even when we feel broken or forgotten, we are seen, known, and claimed by the Creator of the universe.

Jesus Himself drove this home when He told His disciples, "You did not choose Me, but I chose you and appointed you that you should go and bear fruit" (John 15:16, NKJV). His choice is not just about belonging, it's also about purpose. God didn't just call us out of the darkness to sit on the sidelines. He called us to live, to grow, to bear fruit that reflects His love and brings Him glory.

And then there's this beautiful declaration in 1 Peter 2:9 (NKJV): "But you are a chosen generation, a royal priesthood, a holy nation, His own special people, that you may proclaim the praises of Him who called you out of darkness into His marvelous light." I don't know about you, but that takes my breath away every time I read it. We aren't defined by our failures or our pain; we are defined by the God who chose us, loves us, and calls us His own.

Friend, do you see what this means? You are not an accident. You are not a mistake. You are not forgotten. You are chosen, loved, and called by God. Your cracks, your scars, your story, all of it becomes a testimony to His grace when you place it in His hands.

As I began to heal, I kept sensing God nudging me to share my story, not just for my own freedom, but to help others. It wasn't something I ever imagined myself doing. Talking about my abuse felt vulnerable and uncomfortable. But the more I tried to push it away, the stronger the pull became. God didn't want me to hide any longer. He was calling me to use the very thing I thought disqualified me as the very thing that could set others free.

I remember sitting in my living room, feeling completely unqualified to speak publicly about my experience with abuse. At first, I resisted it. I didn't feel qualified. Who was I to stand in front of people and teach, when I had been so broken myself? How could God possibly use my broken story to help others? But then I remembered: God doesn't call the qualified; He qualifies the called. The very thing I thought disqualified me (my pain, my shame, my brokenness) became the exact thing God used to equip me to minister to others. If

God was calling me, then He would give me everything I needed to walk in obedience.

It was shocking to me, after my divorce, when women started sharing with me about their own histories. I heard stories from women who had only recently escaped, and from women that had escaped decades prior. As the years went by, the stories shared with me gave me the courage to stand up and speak against the atrocities of domestic abuse. Those stories woke me up, giving me a realization that abuse needs to be exposed in a way that helps not only those that have experienced abuse, but also those that want to stand in a place of advocacy.

Now, I stand in places I never thought I would: leading seminars, teaching about red flags and green flags in relationships, training others how to recognize the signs of abuse, and training people how to set and maintain healthy boundaries. I help equip people with tools for healing, connecting survivors with local resources and teaching advocates how to take action. I teach well-meaning people what to say and what not to say, because sometimes the smallest words can make the biggest difference.

Through it all, I see God's hand. The cracks in my story have been filled with His golden grace, and now the very places that once felt like shame have become the most powerful parts of my testimony. God kept calling, and when I finally said yes, I discovered that my pain had a purpose. I never imagined that God would use me in a public way, especially when I worked so hard to hide behind the mask.

If God can take my broken story and shape it into a calling, then He can do the same for you. Your purpose may not look like mine, it might not be standing in front of groups or leading seminars (or maybe it is!), but I can promise you this: God has placed something unique within you. He has written a purpose on your life that no one else can fulfill in the exact same way.

So, let me ask you: What is your purpose? What is God calling you to? Maybe He's been nudging you toward something that feels bigger than you are, something that scares you a little, or a lot. Maybe He's asking you to step away from something that no longer serves you, something that has kept you bound. Or maybe, just maybe, He is whispering His golden grace into the empty spaces of your life, inviting you to let Him restore what feels shattered.

Whatever it is, I want you to know this: you are chosen, you are loved, and you are called. The same God who formed you, who knows you by name, is the One who will guide you into your purpose. You don't have to have all the answers right now. You just need to take the next step of faith and trust that the God who began a good work in you will be faithful to complete it.

This is who you are: a child of the King. This is why you are here: to live out the beautiful purpose He designed for you, reflecting His glory through your story.

God doesn't usually reveal our calling in one grand, unmistakable moment. Most often, He begins quietly, in the ordinary rhythms of everyday life. It might be a gentle nudge to reach out to someone who's struggling, a thought that won't leave you about helping in your community, or an idea for a project that aligns with the gifts

He's given you. These small touches, when noticed and acted upon, are often the very first signs of the unique purpose God has for you.

Pay attention to those nudges. God often points us toward opportunities to serve, mentor, or lead in ways that feel natural, because they are tied to the gifts, He's already placed inside of us. You might find that the call isn't always about standing in front of a crowd or leading a large initiative. It could be helping a coworker through a tough project, sitting with someone in grief, offering guidance to a friend navigating a difficult decision, or using your skills in a small group at church. Every small act of faithfulness, done with love, is an opportunity to honor the purpose God has planted within you.

I've seen this in my own life, and in the lives of others. Early on, I didn't know what my calling would involve. It started quietly through sharing my story with a friend, listening to someone who felt isolated, and helping connect women to resources. Each step was a seed God planted.

I've watched others step into leadership in similarly quiet ways:

- A coworker who quietly starts a prayer group at work and discovers her leadership gifts.

- A man who volunteers to mow an elderly neighbor's lawn and learns the joy of serving consistently.

- A woman who writes letters of encouragement to lonely people in her neighborhood and becomes a beacon of hope.

A tiny pebble dropped in a lake can send ripples very far and these small steps are multiplied by God in ways that only He can orchestrate. The key is paying attention and being willing to act. When we notice those nudges and respond in faith, we allow God to show us the gifts He has already placed in our hands and to guide us in using them for His glory.

Everyday Nudges Toward Your Calling

As you look at your own life, notice the small ways God is already nudging you, those moments where your gifts, your compassion, your wisdom, or your skills meet a need. These everyday opportunities are not random; they are clues to the purpose He has designed for you. Each act of service, each word of encouragement, each step of faith is part of a larger story that God is writing through you. Your purpose may not be revealed all at once, but as you respond to these small nudges with obedience and trust, God will gradually unfold the path He has prepared. Step forward, even in small ways, and watch how He uses your life (your story, your gifts, your heart) to bring light, hope, and transformation to the world around you.

You weren't put here by accident. God has a purpose for your life, and He's inviting you to step into it, one small step at a time. And even when the path seems uncertain, even when you feel unqualified, God is at work behind the scenes. As Romans 8:28-30 (NKJV) reminds us:

"And we know that all things work together for good to those who love God, to those who are called according to His purpose. For whom He foreknew, He also predestined to be conformed to the image of His Son... Moreover, whom He predestined, these He also called; whom He called, these He also justified; and whom He justified, these He also glorified."

God's calling is not random. He sees your journey through the twists, the hardships, and the victories, and He will continue to guide you. You are formed according to His purpose, chosen to reflect His image, and called to share His gospel to the world. The steps you take, no matter how small, are part of the path He has laid out for you. Trust Him, lean into His guidance, and step forward with confidence, knowing that the God who began a good work in you will faithfully carry it to completion.

Chapter Gate Reminder:
The following chapter continues anonymized, paraphrased recollections intended to protect privacy.

Chapter 8: Guardrails of Grace

A fence is not built to control your neighbor, but to protect the privacy and peace of your space. Boundaries work the same way. They are not walls of control meant to keep people under your rule, but safeguards to protect what is valuable in your life: your peace, your dignity, your healing. The people that protest your boundaries are usually the same ones who benefited the most when you had none. Setting healthy limits is not selfish, it is stewardship of your heart and your life.

The word "boundary" often gets a bad reputation. People may call you controlling, rigid, or cold when you begin to draw lines where there were previously none. But that reaction says far more about them than it does about you. Healthy boundaries are never about punishment or power. They are about clarity, safety, and freedom. They create space for love to grow without being trampled by manipulation or misuse.

For survivors of abuse, boundaries can feel especially complicated. Years of being silenced, controlled, or shamed can make it hard to know where someone else ends and your free will begins. You may feel guilty for saying no, or fearful of how someone might react if you speak up. You may not even know where to begin setting limits to the access other people have to you and your decisions. But boundaries are not about rejection, they are about direction. They are an act of reclaiming the voice God gave you and the life He intends for you to live.

Learning to set boundaries is part of healing. It is part of saying, "I matter. My needs matter. My safety matters." And that shift can be life-changing. In this chapter, we will explore why boundaries are necessary, how to recognize when they are missing, and how to begin building them in ways that honor both your faith and your future.

For years, I avoided setting boundaries, afraid of reactions, and afraid of being seen as controlling. After my divorce, I realized my lack of boundaries was not protecting me, it continued to endanger my emotional and physical safety.

My motivation to set boundaries finally came one weekend at church. While I was in another part of the building, my kids ran into a friend of mine. She and I had been friends for many years, and I had always trusted her. But that day, she began sharing details about my children's father, his remarriage, and what she knew about his new wife. At that time, my teenagers had only just discovered through social media that their dad had remarried. In the few texts he would send throughout the year, he hadn't shared anything about dating someone, let alone about his remarriage. So, having someone want to talk to them about their father's remarriage, in the middle of the church hallway, with people passing by, was deeply uncomfortable for them.

After we left church, my kids told me what had happened. I reached out to her and gently explained that conversations about their father's private life had to be off-limits. It was too painful for them, especially when they were not included in this newest milestone. And having that conversation in the middle of the church as people walked by wasn't the right place to approach it. Instead of understanding, she told me I was trying to control what she talked about.

A few weeks later, she tried again. She approached my kids, asking them questions about their father that she knew they wouldn't have the answers to. My kids were uneasy and unsettled by her probing. That was the moment I realized boundaries were no longer optional, they were necessary. But this time I didn't shy away from boundary setting because I was doing it for my kids. Grace still guided my response, but this time, it came with consequences.

I had already explained the boundary. Now it was time to act on it. I didn't make a scene or cut ties dramatically. I simply stopped initiating contact. When she texted me weeks later, asking why I had not texted or called, I calmly explained that she had pushed through a very firm boundary. I let her know that I didn't trust her anymore and I needed some space.

Looking back, this was a turning point for me. Setting boundaries doesn't have to be dramatic or angry. It can be as simple as deciding what is and isn't acceptable and following through consistently. I realized that protecting my children, and my own peace, wasn't about being controlling. It was about being a good steward for myself and my children and loving in a way that mattered to our little family.

Maybe you've been in a situation where someone pushes past your limits, and you feel guilty for speaking up. I want you to hear this clearly: boundaries are not unkind. They are an act of caring for yourself and for those you love. Saying "this is off-limits" or "this isn't okay" isn't a rejection; it's a declaration that your emotional and spiritual well-being matters. And sometimes, it also means stepping back from people who can't respect those limits.

It wasn't easy at first, and I'll be honest, it still feels uncomfortable for me at times. Learning to set boundaries is a lot like going to the gym after years of being a couch potato. The process feels awkward and intimidating at first, it can be painful and also feel good at the same time. The relief, the clarity, and the peace that comes when you hold firm on your boundaries is worth every uncomfortable moment that comes before it.

Why Boundaries Matter

The Bible gives us a clear blueprint for the importance of protecting our hearts. Proverbs 4:23 (NKJV) says, *"Guard your heart with all diligence, for out of it spring the issues of life."* This verse reminds us that our hearts are not just emotional centers, they are the wellspring of our thoughts, words, and actions. When we allow unchecked access to our hearts, whether through toxic relationships, manipulation, harmful patterns, or well-meaning people that step past the line, we open the door to confusion, pain, and compromise. Setting boundaries is one way we guard our hearts, honoring God's design for our emotional, spiritual, and relational well-being.

Boundaries are not about selfishness or trying to control others. They are about stewardship. God calls us to manage what is entrusted to us, including our emotions, time, and energy. Just as a gardener prunes plants to encourage healthy growth, we prune relationships and situations that threaten our peace or interfere with our calling. A boundary can be as simple as saying no to a request that drains us, stepping back from a relationship that consistently harms, or refusing to engage in gossip or manipulation. Each of these acts is an exercise in protecting the life and energy God has entrusted to you.

Understanding the Biblical call to guard our hearts helps us see that boundaries are not optional, they are essential. But knowing why boundaries matter is only the first step. The real challenge comes in putting them into practice in everyday life. How do we protect our hearts while still showing love and grace? How do we honor God's design without feeling guilty or harsh?

The answer lies in practical, intentional boundaries. These are the day-to-day limits we set to preserve our peace, protect our families, and honor God in our relationships. They may look different for each person, but the principle is the same: creating clear lines that safeguard our hearts while still allowing room for healthy connection, growth, and faith.

I learned a lot about boundaries through my professional experience and while I pursued my master's degree. In those environments, the rules were clear. I took classes on management and leadership that included learning how to teach and implement healthy boundary setting. Deadlines, responsibilities, and professional expectations created natural boundaries, and following them felt straightforward. Saying no to extra assignments I didn't have time for, delegating tasks, or asking for clarification on my role didn't feel uncomfortable, it was expected. In many ways, work gave me permission to set limits, and I thrived in that structure.

Personal life, however, was a different story. Saying no to family members, friends, or even acquaintances felt heavier, more emotional, and somehow guilt-laden. There were no job descriptions or official policies to lean on. Every boundary felt like a negotiation, an emotional tug-of-war where I worried about hurting feelings, being seen as controlling, or causing conflict. The truth is, personal boundaries require the same courage, clarity, and self-respect that professional boundaries do, but they are harder because they touch the heart, not just the schedule.

Over time, I realized that the skills I practiced in work and school (communicating expectations clearly, protecting my time, holding others accountable when boundaries were crossed) could be translated into my personal life. I just had to allow myself to apply them, without guilt, in relationships where emotions run deeper and stakes feel higher. Gradually, I began to see that the principles of respect, responsibility, and clarity are universal; they work in classrooms, offices, homes, and hearts alike.

Practical Examples of Boundaries

1. **Emotional Boundaries**: Choosing not to engage in conversations that are hurtful, manipulative, or gossipy to others. Making certain topics off-limits to people that don't have any stake, or involvement, in the topic. Protecting your heart by deciding what emotions you will carry for others and what you release to God.

2. **Time Boundaries**: Saying no to commitments that overwhelm you or pull you away from your family, rest, or spiritual growth. Allocating time intentionally for what matters most. This includes church responsibilities. It's ok to say no, God is not calling you to hold up the church on your shoulders alone.

3. **Physical Boundaries**: Maintaining personal space and privacy, especially in situations where others may disregard your comfort or safety. This might look like deciding who you do and do not allow to come through your front door.

4. **Relational Boundaries**: Limiting contact with individuals who repeatedly disrespect your values, your family, or your peace. This may include temporarily or permanently stepping back from certain friendships or family members.

5. **Digital Boundaries**: Managing social media or phone interactions to avoid exposure to negativity, gossip, bullying, or manipulation. Hiding people on your feed that are emotionally draining. Choosing when, how, and how long you engage online.

6. **Spiritual Boundaries**: Protecting your spiritual life by choosing when to participate in discussions, events, or environments that make you feel unsafe or could undermine your faith, lead you into compromise, or distract from your calling.

In essence, boundaries matter because they protect the heart, preserve the soul, and allow God's best for our lives to take root. They are an act of faith as much as an act of self-care. They are an acknowledgment that God's design for us includes both love and limits, grace and structure. By holding firm on boundaries, we honor God, ourselves, and the people He has placed in our lives.

Breaking the Lies

When it comes to boundaries, there are many lies and misconceptions that can make us hesitate to set them. Some of the most common myths are that boundaries are unloving, selfish, or inconsistent with God's will. Others tell us that as Christians, we must always sacrifice, always give, and never say no. These lies can keep us trapped in unhealthy relationships, patterns of guilt, and emotional exhaustion. It's time to break those lies and see boundaries for what they truly are: a form of love and stewardship, both for ourselves and for others.

Myth #1: God wants me to always sacrifice.

While Scripture encourages generosity and service, it never calls us to abuse, neglect, or to endanger ourselves in the name of obedience or submission. Jesus Himself balanced giving with rest and discernment. In Matthew 11:28-30, He says, *"Come to Me, all who labor and are heavy laden, and I will give you rest. Take My yoke upon you and learn from Me, for I am gentle and lowly in heart, and you will find rest for your souls. For My yoke is easy and My burden is light."* God's call is not to constant self-neglect, but to stewardship of the life, energy, and heart He has entrusted to you. Setting boundaries is part of carrying your "yoke" wisely, not living under an unbearable one.

Myth #2: Boundaries push people away.

Some people fear that enforcing limits will drive loved ones away or damage relationships permanently. But Scripture teaches that accountability, respect, and honesty are the foundations of healthy connections. Galatians 6:5 reminds us, *"For each will have to bear his own load."* When we set boundaries, we are not punishing others, we are giving them the space and responsibility to walk in their own path while protecting our peace. In many cases, healthy boundaries strengthen relationships, creating trust and respect where there may have been confusion, resentment, or chaos.

Myth #3: Boundaries are a lack of faith.

Some believe that to enforce boundaries is to rely on their own strength rather than trusting God. But Proverbs 16:3 tells us, *"Commit your works to the Lord, and your plans will be established."* Setting limits is not a sign of mistrust in God, it is a way of acknowledging His provision and wisdom in our lives. By creating healthy boundaries, we recognize that our lives, relationships, and energy are sacred and worthy of care, and we are partnering with God to steward them well.

Myth #4: Boundaries are unloving.

Many people worry that saying no, limiting contact, or enforcing rules in relationships makes them appear harsh or unkind. But boundaries are actually a form of love. Boundaries help to support relationships that are healthy, respectful, and mutually beneficial. Without limits, love can easily be taken for granted or misused. True love honors both the other person and you, and that requires clear lines. Jesus often lovingly implemented his own boundaries.

****

Breaking these lies is liberating. Boundaries are not acts of selfishness, fear, or pride, they are acts of courage, faith, and love.

They help us live fully in the freedom God intends, protecting our hearts while still allowing us to serve, love, and give generously in ways that are sustainable and honor Him.

Jesus as Our Example of Boundaries

If you still feel torn about whether boundaries are truly Christlike, look at the way Jesus lived. He was full of compassion and mercy, yet He also knew when to say no, when to walk away, and when to rest. His life shows us that boundaries are not only wise but holy.

- **He withdrew for rest and prayer.** Crowds pressed in constantly, yet Jesus "often withdrew to lonely places and prayed" (Luke 5:16). He knew that to pour out, He first had to be filled by the Father. This shows us the importance of guarding time for rest and renewal.

- **He didn't meet every demand.** In John 11, when Lazarus was sick, Jesus did not rush immediately at others' request but followed the Father's timing. He was not driven by guilt or pressure but by obedience.

- **He refused to engage in unhealthy conversations.** When the Pharisees tried to trap Him, He often answered with silence or a question of His own (Matthew 21:23-27). He did not let others manipulate Him into their agendas.

- **He defined relationships clearly.** Jesus loved the crowds, but He spent most of His time with the twelve, and even within that, He drew closest to Peter, James, and John. He showed us that intimacy requires discernment, not unlimited access.

- **He walked away when necessary.** At times, when the crowds became hostile or when His hour had not yet come, He "slipped away" (John 8:59). Boundaries protected His mission and His life until the cross.

Jesus shows us that boundaries are not selfish, they are strategic and Spirit-led. He modeled balance, serving with love, but also resting, stepping back, and refusing to be controlled. If the Son of God Himself set limits while walking in perfect love, then we too can follow His example without guilt.

Practical Tools for Boundary Setting

Knowing that boundaries matter is one thing; living them out in daily life is another thing. If you're like me, you've probably experienced the tug-of-war between wanting to protect your peace and fearing that someone will accuse you of being harsh, selfish, or unloving. The good news is, boundaries don't have to be complicated. With a few practical tools, you can begin to create healthy rhythms that honor God, protect your heart, and strengthen your relationships. Here are a few practical tools:

1. Get Clear on Your Limits

Before you can communicate boundaries, you have to know what they are. Take time to prayerfully reflect on where you feel drained, unsafe, or disrespected. These are clues that a boundary may be needed. Proverbs 14:15 (NKJV) reminds us, *"The simple believe every word, but the prudent considers well his steps."* Clarity and discernment equal wisdom. Write down your personal non-negotiables, whether it's protecting your time with your children, saying no to gossip, or limiting emotional exhaustion in relationships that take but never give.

2. Use Simple, Honest Language

Boundaries don't need to be long explanations, and you don't need to apologize when implementing them. In fact, the simpler and calmer, the better. A few examples:

- "I'm not available for that."
- "I'm not going to discuss that topic."
- "I can't stay longer than an hour."
- "I need to step back from this conversation."

3. Expect Resistance Without Losing Peace

When you first begin setting boundaries, some people may resist, especially if they have benefited from your lack of them. This does not mean your boundaries are wrong. It means they are working. Stay calm, stay consistent, and don't feel pressured to over-explain. Philippians 4:7 promises, *"And the peace of God, which surpasses all understanding, will guard your hearts and minds through Christ Jesus."* Let the peace that God gives you guard your heart, even when others don't understand.

4. Follow Through with Consequences

A boundary without follow-through is just a wish. If someone continually ignores your limits, you most likely need to take further steps, stepping back from the relationship, limiting time spent together, or involving accountability if necessary. This is not about punishment; it's stewardship. Think of it as reinforcing the fence around your garden so that what's precious inside stays safe.

5. Start Small and Build Confidence

You don't have to overhaul your entire life at once. Start with one small boundary in an area where you feel safe practicing. Maybe it's saying no to one extra responsibility this week or not answering work emails after a set hour. It could mean not answering the phone when you're spending quality time with your children, no matter what expectation the person calling has. Each time you follow through, you'll gain confidence that you can honor your limits without guilt.

6. Lean on Support and Accountability

Boundary-setting can feel lonely, but you don't have to do it alone. Find safe friends, mentors, or a counselor who will remind you that boundaries are healthy and God-honoring. Proverbs 15:22 says, *"Without counsel, plans go awry, but in the multitude of counselors they are established."* Having support keeps you from slipping back into old patterns when guilt or pushback comes.

Boundaries are not a one-time decision but a lifestyle of protecting what God has entrusted to you. The more you practice these tools, the more natural it will feel to guard your heart with diligence while still walking in love. Boundaries make room for freedom, peace, and healthier connections.

The Fruit of Boundaries

When we first start setting boundaries, it can feel uncomfortable, even scary. We worry about what others will think or how they'll respond. But over time, healthy boundaries begin to produce fruit, visible evidence of God's wisdom at work in our lives. Just as a garden thrives when its plants are protected, watered, pruned, and weeded, our hearts and relationships flourish when we guard them well.

1. Peace

Boundaries create peace in places where there was once chaos. By setting limits, we create a safe place for our souls, a quiet space where God's presence can settle us. Instead of constantly reacting to other people's demands, we learn to live from a place of calm and clarity.

2. Freedom

Ironically, limits bring freedom. When we are not weighed down by guilt, manipulation, or constant people-pleasing, we are free to say yes to what truly matters. Galatians 5:1 (NKJV) declares, *"It is for freedom that Christ has set us free. Stand firm, then, and do not let yourselves be burdened again by a yoke of slavery."* Boundaries break the chains of unhealthy expectations and allow us to walk freely in God's calling.

3. Healthier Relationships

Boundaries sift out relationships built on control or exploitation and nurture those built on mutual respect and love. Proverbs 17:17 (NKJV) says, *"A friend loves at all times, and a brother is born for adversity."* The people that love us will love us at all times and stand with us through adversity. When we enforce healthy limits, we make space for relationships that are genuine, supportive, and enduring. Some connections may fall away, but what remains is healthier and stronger.

4. Emotional and Spiritual Growth

Boundaries protect the soil of our hearts so that God's Word can take root and grow. Jesus said in John 15:5 (NKJV), *"I am the vine, you are the branches. He who abides in Me, and I in him, bears much fruit."* By guarding our hearts, we are able to stay connected to Christ without constant distraction or depletion. This makes room for maturity, resilience, and a deeper walk with God.

5. Protection for the Next Generation

When we model healthy boundaries, we teach our children and those around us that it's possible to live with both love and wisdom. They learn by watching us that "no" can be just as holy as "yes," and that protecting one's heart is not selfish but Biblical. In this way, boundaries are not only for our own well-being, but also a legacy for those who come after us.

The fruit of boundaries is life-giving. Peace, freedom, stronger relationships, spiritual growth, and protection for future generations all flow from the courage to say, "This is where I end and you begin." Boundaries are not about shutting people out; they are about creating the space for love, respect, and faith to grow.

****

Setting boundaries is not easy. It requires courage to speak truth, strength to follow through, and faith to trust God with the outcomes. You may encounter pushback or be misunderstood but remember that boundaries are not walls to shut people out, they are gates that let in what is good and keep out what is emotionally or physically draining or harmful to you and your family. They are one of the ways we guard our hearts so that we can remain healthy, whole, and able to love as God designed.

As you begin to walk this out, give yourself grace. Boundaries are a process, not a one-time event. Some days you may stumble or feel guilty but keep going. Every small step you take toward honoring your limits is a step toward peace, freedom, and healthier relationships. The fruit will come, because God blesses our obedience to His calling.

Boundaries are hard. Learning to recognize them, honor them, and put them into practice can feel overwhelming, especially after years of living in a world where your needs and safety were not respected. This chapter ends with a prayer because setting boundaries is not just a practical exercise, it is a spiritual one. Asking God for strength, clarity, and courage reminds us that we are not meant to navigate this alone. Prayer invites His presence into the difficult work of protecting our hearts, our time, and our peace, giving us the courage to take the next step, however small, toward freedom and wholeness.

Prayer

Lord,

Thank You for the gift of wisdom and the reminder that my heart is worth guarding. Help me to walk in courage as I set boundaries, not from fear or selfishness, but from love and obedience to You. When I feel guilty or misunderstood, remind me that my worth is not defined by the approval of others but by Your truth.

Teach me to say *yes* to Your call and *no* when it is wise, so that my life reflects balance, peace, and strength. Protect my children, my family, and my relationships, and let the fruit of healthy boundaries be evident in every area of my life. May my "yes" be wholehearted, and my "no" be steady, always rooted in grace and truth.

In Jesus' name, Amen.

Chapter Gate Reminder:
The following chapter continues anonymized, paraphrased recollections intended to protect privacy.

Chapter 9: Why Did She Stay?

"Why did you stay so long?"

It's the question survivors are asked more than almost any other. Sometimes this question comes from someone that doesn't know the survivor well and is just curious about why someone would stay in an abusive situation. Sometimes this question comes from people who care, people who genuinely want to understand. They can't wrap their minds around why someone would stay in a relationship that's clearly causing so much pain. Their intentions might be kind, but their words land heavily. And sometimes the question comes from people that are judgmental and look down their noses at a woman that stayed in a dysfunctional and abusive relationship because they are certain they would have made *better* choices.

And almost without fail, the question of why someone stayed is followed by a statement, one that cuts just a little bit deeper:

"I would have left the moment I even suspected abuse was coming."

At first glance, these might sound like simple things an onlooker might say, but to a survivor, these sentiments often land like accusations. They carry an unspoken judgment, either that her story must not be as serious as she claims, or that she was too weak to do what needed to be done. The reality is, no one knows how they would handle an abusive situation until they have personally experienced it. And even then, each situation is nuanced.

Abuse is not that simple.

What people don't realize is that leaving doesn't happen in a moment, it's a process. It's a thousand small calculations of risk and safety, of fear and hope. When someone asks why she stayed, what she often hears instead is, *you should have known better.* But survivors stay because they are trying to survive, because love, fear, faith, children, finances, or sheer uncertainty make the way out feel more dangerous than the life they already know.

How do you explain coercive control to someone who's never experienced it? How do you describe the slow erosion of self-worth, the manipulation that starts as something so subtle you barely notice it until it becomes the air you breathe? Those tactics often begin as small seeds disguised as concern, affection, or protection, and grow over time into a web of control and fear that's nearly impossible to escape.

And even when a survivor does find their voice, they walk a tightrope. Every word they share, even after escaping, carries weight and risk. How much can they say without those words getting back to their abuser? How do they tell their story honestly while still keeping themselves safe?

So many abusers work hard to control the story even after the relationship ends. Abusers spread lies, twisting the truth to make themselves look innocent and their partner appear unstable or fully at fault for the marriage ending. And when a survivor dares to correct that false narrative, the threats often follow, threats of legal action, harm, or further damage to their reputation.

So, many survivors stay silent. They stop defending themselves, not because the lies are true, but because the fight is exhausting and dangerous. They retreat, quietly leaving their church, pulling away from friends, and fading from the places where they once felt seen.

That's why I want to answer this question *"Why did you stay so long?"* as honestly as I can in this chapter. My hope is to begin untangling the complex web that keeps someone bound in an abusive relationship.

Before we dive in to the reasons why women stay, I want to share a message with the survivors reading this:

Dear Survivor,

If you are reading this and seeing pieces of your own story in these pages, I need you to hear me clearly: you are brave. You are not weak for using the tools you had to survive. You are not foolish. You did what you had to do to make it through every day, to protect yourself and your children, to preserve some sense of peace in a world that offered you none. That is strength.

I know how heavy this all feels, how shame and fear can tangle together until you can hardly breathe. But please know this: you are not alone. You have walked through something that would have broken many, and yet here you are, still seeking truth, still reaching for hope, still reading words that hold both pain and promise. That is courage.

I am proud of you, not just for surviving, but for daring to understand, to see the patterns clearly, to believe there is more ahead than fear and control. Healing takes time, but the fact that you're here means you've already begun.

****

As I sat thinking about a succinct way to explain why I stayed, my thoughts went to what's often called the "boiled frog" analogy. If you drop a frog into boiling water, it will jump out right away. But if you place it in cool water and slowly turn up the heat, it won't notice the danger until it's too late. As grim as that image sounds, it's one of the clearest ways I can describe what happens in abuse. The temperature rises so slowly, so subtly, that by the time the survivor realizes what's happening, they're already in too deep: isolated, confused, and trying to survive one small moment at a time.

Abuse is rarely loud at first. It doesn't always look like bruises or fits of rage. More often, it begins quietly through subtle words and gradual shifts in power that grow stronger over time. By the time a survivor realizes what's happening, they're usually trapped in a web of confusion, fear, and dependency that's been carefully spun.

Abusers rely on a variety of tools to maintain control, each one tightening the hold a little more until escape feels impossible. Understanding these methods helps us see why survivors stay, and why getting out is never as simple as it sounds.

Isolation

This tool that an abuser uses is almost invisible. At first, it looks like love and concern. The statements an abuser uses seem like they are made in an effort to protect you or allow more time together. Statements like: "Your friend is a bad influence." "I just want you all to myself." "We don't need friends in our life, we have each other." "Your friends don't really understand us." These statements might feel protective and loving at first. But they eventually turn into much more overt ways of isolating and controlling. She's no longer *allowed* to be on the phone with a friend or family member when he's home. Family gatherings are "too far" or "too loud" or a host of other *reasons.*

Slowly, the survivor's world begins to shrink. Phone calls stop. Invitations get turned down. Church can feel uncomfortable because he doesn't like the people there, but he may insist the family still attend, badmouthing the people that are kind when they pull out of the parking lot. Family visits become tense because defenses are up to protect the perfect facade. Eventually, the survivor finds herself alone, cut off from her support system, from the people who might notice what's happening. Isolation is one of the abuser's most powerful tactics because it removes outside voices that could speak truth or offer perspective.

For me, the isolation started willingly. I thought I was protecting him, protecting *us*. I began pulling away from friends, especially the ones who might have seen through the façade. I told myself it was an act of love, that if I just showed enough loyalty and care, he would finally feel secure enough to change.

But over the years, as his treatment of me intensified, I realized that no matter how hard I tried, it wasn't changing him. Something inside me began to wither. I started believing the words he used to tear me down, that I was too emotional, too difficult, too much. The more I withdrew, the smaller I became. And the more I believed his version of who I was, the more I accepted the world he created for me.

I kept some people at arm's length because of what he thought of them. I filtered my choices through his opinions and reactions.

Slowly, my world became centered around keeping peace and avoiding conflict.

Then something subtle began to shift. The more alone I felt, the more I looked to him for validation, direction, and identity. He noticed it. When someone would ask me a question, my eyes would instinctively turn to him before I answered, as if seeking silent permission. And when I finally realized what I was doing and how much of myself I had given away, I stopped looking at him for confirmation before I would speak. He noticed that, too.

Financial Control

Money becomes another weapon. Sometimes it's subtle, "I'll handle the bills; you're not good with numbers." Other times it's blatant like taking her paycheck. Sometimes it shows up as a budget that is so restrictive she's put on a cash-only basis with no access to accounts. And the cash he gives her is barely enough to cover groceries. She may be forbidden to work altogether.

Many survivors have shared with me that credit cards and loans were taken out in their names, yet they had no access to the funds. Sometimes they were aware of the accounts but were told it was for "family finances" or for "the family business." Other times, it was done entirely in secret, and they didn't discover the truth until after they left, when they checked their credit and realized it had been completely overextended or ruined.

Leaving becomes a nearly impossible choice. How do you walk away when you have no savings and no credit? How can you support yourself and the children depending on you? Financial control ensures that even when a survivor comes through the fog and realizes she's in an abusive relationship, she's trapped by practical realities. The abuser knows this and counts on it.

The financial needs on the path to freedom seem insurmountable. *How can I provide a stable home when every apartment requires a credit check? How can I provide transportation when every vehicle owned is only in his name? How can I put food on the table without a job? How can I clothe my kids? How will I keep the lights on and the water running if I do find a place to live? How can I find a job without recent work experience? If I can find a job, what will I do about childcare?*

And the list goes on. There are so many big and small financial needs that create one big tangled web that keeps someone in an abusive relationship.

Emotional Manipulation

This is perhaps the most confusing tool of all. Abusers twist emotions until up feels like down and wrong feels right. They gaslight (twisting the truth and denying what was said or done) until a survivor begins to doubt her own memory and sanity. They shift blame with words like, "You made me do this." "If you hadn't said (or done) that, I wouldn't have gotten angry." "If you had just handled it the way I wanted you to, I wouldn't have to manage you."

Over time, these phrases, and hundreds like them, teach a survivor to walk on eggshells, constantly anticipating moods and avoiding triggers just to keep the peace. She begins to believe that maybe it really *is* her fault, that if she were more loving, more patient, or less sensitive, things would somehow get better.

She learns to read every movement, every sigh, every micro expression, as if decoding a language only she can understand. She learns that when he uses the word *manage* its code for punishment, that silence can be louder than shouting, and that one wrong glance can change the whole tone of the day.

Emotional manipulation is so insidious, so cruelly effective, that trying to explain it in a few paragraphs feels like an injustice. There is so much more I could write about emotional manipulation. There's enough to fill a bookshelf, and still, it wouldn't fully capture what it does to a survivor's heart. It slowly erodes self-esteem, courage, and confidence until she no longer recognizes the person she once was.

Spiritual Manipulation

I know we talked about this earlier in the Faith Untangled chapter, but it's worth repeating here as part of the answer to "why did you stay so long?" For many Christian women, this form of control cuts the deepest. Sometimes the spouse professes to be a "Christian" and sometimes the spouse is not a believer but uses Bible verses against their believing wife, twisting scripture to justify dominance. "Wives, submit to your husbands" is a verse often used, while conveniently ignoring the verses about love, respect, and mutual care. An abuser may weaponize forgiveness, insisting that "a good Christian wife" should pray more, endure more, and never speak out. He considers her silence a virtue.

When faith becomes a tool of control, it not only traps the survivor but distorts her relationship with God. She may begin to wonder if God Himself is disappointed in her for wanting to leave. This spiritual confusion can paralyze her, keeping her in bondage long after she recognizes the abuse.

The Children

So many of us stay because of the children. We tell ourselves that as long as everyone is under the same roof, we can protect them. We can absorb the blows, whether physical or emotional. We can take the tension and walk on eggshells if it means keeping them safe.

Abuse rewires a mother's instincts. What should be simple, protecting your children, becomes twisted in a world ruled by fear and manipulation. Every decision feels like a gamble. If I stay, I can intercept the anger and defuse it before it reaches them. If I leave, he will still have time alone with them, and I won't be there to protect them when the door closes. These thoughts kept me up at night. Would the abuse shift to them after the separation?

And sometimes, the abuser begins turning the children against their mother long before she even leaves. He mocks her in front of them, calls her names, and critiques everything she does, from how she folds the laundry to the meal she cooks and everything in between. Slowly, he plants seeds of doubt in their minds, painting her as too sensitive, too controlling, or too foolish for the children to take seriously. Over time, those small digs erode not only her confidence but also the way her children see her. It's one of the most painful forms of betrayal, watching the people you love most start to believe the lies spoken about you.

These are the impossible choices survivors face. To the outside world, it looks like she's choosing him over her children. But in her mind, she's choosing safety, the only kind she can control. The abuser knows this, too. He uses the children as leverage, twisting her love for them into another form of control. "You'll destroy the family," he says. "They need their father." "You'll never see them again if you walk out the door." "You can leave, but you'll never take *MY* kids with you." And for a long time, she believes his messaging.

But the truth is, the children are already affected in ways she can't even imagine. They have already lost their "family." They feel the tension even when no words are spoken. They learn to read the air, to tiptoe through moods. They carry fear even when no hand is raised. What a mother thinks she's containing; the children are inhaling quietly day after day.

Monitoring and Tracking

Today's technology has made it easier than ever for abusers to monitor and track their partners, extending their control far beyond the walls of the home. I've heard countless stories from women who discovered they were being tracked in ways they never imagined: tiny Apple Air Tags slipped into purses, diaper bags, or car seats; hidden tracking apps secretly installed on phones or tablets; even "safety" or "family" apps used as tools of surveillance. Not to mention the apps that are specifically designed for your vehicle with services like locking, unlocking, remote start, and location tracking.

What might look harmless or even helpful on the surface, like a location-sharing feature, or a car manufacturer's app can become another way for an abuser to tighten his grip. He always knows where she is, how long she stayed there, and who she visited. If she has access to a credit or debit card, he can set up instant notifications to his phone, alerting him every time a transaction is made and showing exactly where and when it happened. Sometimes he even knows what she bought, with the right retail store apps. Even her attempts to buy gas, groceries, or a bus ticket can become a trail of breadcrumbs leading straight back to her.

And this doesn't even take into consideration what happens when an abuser feels his control slipping through his fingers. If he suspects she's finding ways around his tracking, he will often recruit others to help, calling her friends or family members to "check up" on her under the guise of concern, or accusing her of dodging his devices and hiding her location. In reality, these are just more layers of surveillance, making her feel like there's no safe corner left, no one she can trust.

The result is a chilling kind of omnipresence. Even when he isn't physically there, she feels him hovering over every move, every decision, every mile she drives. Technology and manipulation become invisible chains, reinforcing the message he's already drilled into her: "You can't get away. I'll always control you."

Fear and Threats

Fear is the thread that ties all of these tools together. Sometimes it's physical, a look, a slammed door, a hand raised just high enough to make the point, a shove, a slap, a punch. Other times, it's psychological threats: taking the children, ruining her reputation through false accusations, harming a pet, or harming himself if she leaves.

The goal is always the same: to keep the survivor controlled, compliant, and afraid of what might come next. In truth, the fear of what's *coming* is often more powerful than the violence itself. Physical wounds can heal, but the anticipation of danger lingers, reshaping how a survivor moves through every moment of her day. It changes the way she breathes, the way she walks through a room, the way she reads every sound and expression.

Fear becomes the background noise of her life. It's a constant humming, invisible to everyone else but deafening to her. It rewires her brain for survival, not logic. Rational thought is replaced by instinct. Every decision is filtered through two questions: "What will happen if I make him angry?" and "How can I keep the situation calm?"

Over time, fear becomes its own form of invisible imprisonment. It doesn't need chains or locks. It lives inside her, making her second-guess every word, every glance, every plan to leave. The unpredictability of the abuse keeps her on edge, teaching her that safety isn't found in escape - it's found in managing the danger. So, she stays, not because she wants to, but because fear convinces her it's the only way to survive.

Confusion

The cruelest part of abuse is that it doesn't happen all the time. There are good days, sometimes even wonderful days, that make the survivor believe change is possible. She replays them in her mind, wondering what she did differently, thinking maybe if she could just replicate those moments leading up to the good times, she could make the calm last.

Some abusers offer apologies, maybe even tears. "It will never happen again," they promise, and for a little while, things are peaceful. These brief moments of tenderness create confusion and false hope. The survivor clings to the memory of who he used to be, believing that if she loves him better, prays harder, or forgives more, she can bring that version of him back. His unstable behavior keeps her off balance and trapped, always waiting for the man she first fell in love with to return.

Other abusers never apologize. They go silent, brooding, visibly carrying the weight of the imagined slights committed against them. Sometimes, they even demand an apology from their spouse, forcing her to take responsibility for the chaos she did not cause.

Whether through fleeting tenderness or cold control, the effect is the same: the survivor's emotions are manipulated, and she is kept in a state of confusion. Her mind is constantly evaluating every interaction, and her hope and fear are perpetually tangled together.

****

Each of these tools works together to create an invisible prison, one without walls, yet made of fear, confusion, and dependence. From the outside, it might look like the survivor is choosing to stay. From the inside, it feels like she's doing everything she can to survive. This is what keeps her bound in the very web of control she longs to escape.

I want to be very clear: these are just a few of the tactics used. There are countless ways abusers keep a survivor afraid and stuck. She is well aware that staying doesn't guarantee safety, but she also understands that leaving opens up a door to the unknown and the potential for a different kind of danger. Freedom often comes with risk, but it also opens the door to healing, to showing ourselves and our children what courage looks like, and to breaking the patterns that have held us hostage.

Abuse thrives in silence, but truth brings light to the darkness. As Luke 12:2-3 (NKJV) tells us, "For there is nothing covered that will not be revealed, nor hidden that will not be known. Therefore, whatever you have spoken in the dark will be heard in the light, and what you have spoken in the ear in inner rooms will be proclaimed on the housetops." This verse is a clear reminder that the darkness cannot last forever, what is hidden will eventually be brought into the light, and truth has the power to break the hold of secrecy and fear.

Understanding how abusers operate doesn't just explain why she stayed, it reveals the depth of her resilience, the countless ways she survived in a world designed to break her.

If you are that survivor, I pray these words help you see that your story is not one of weakness, but of strength. If you are someone walking beside her, my hope is that you carry this truth with you: love and truth together have the power to untangle even the most intricate web. Freedom is not instant, but it is possible.

To those who are walking alongside a survivor (a friend, pastor, counselor, or loved one) please know that nothing written in these pages will surprise her. The descriptions here will not frighten her, because she already knows them by heart. She's lived them.

What she needs most is not your shock or pity but your steadiness. She needs a safe place where she doesn't have to explain or defend what happened. She needs patience when her progress feels slow, understanding when fear still lingers, and compassion when trust comes hard.

Your presence matters more than your words. When you listen without judgment, when you remind her that what happened was not her fault, when you simply hold space for her story, you become part of her healing.

Chapter Gate Reminder:
The following chapter continues anonymized, paraphrased recollections intended to protect privacy.

Chapter 10: How to Help Without Hurting

Good intentions aren't good enough. This point is so important that I'm going to say it again. Meaning well doesn't always mean you're doing well. I know those statements seem harsh, but when it comes to walking with someone who has experienced abuse, someone's good intentions can still cause very deep harm.

We often explain away hurtful good intentions by saying, "Aw, their heart was in the right place." But in doing so, we minimize the hurt of a survivor by justifying the words of the one who caused the pain. We assume that sincerity automatically equals safety, but it doesn't. A person can mean well and still say something that deepens a survivor's shame, questions their faith, or causes them to retreat back into silence.

The truth is that love without understanding can unintentionally wound. A compassionate heart is a beautiful starting point, but it's not the finish line. Helping well requires awareness, sensitivity, and wisdom that can only come through education, understanding, prayer, and open communication. It means learning what abuse really looks like, what trauma does to the mind and body, and how words and actions can either build trust or destroy it.

When we take time to learn, we begin to see that helping someone come out of abuse is a tender space. It's not about fixing, rescuing, or offering quick, uninformed solutions. It's about listening, believing, and walking gently beside someone who has known deep fear and pain. That kind of help doesn't come naturally; it comes through humility, education, and a willingness to be taught how to love like Jesus loves: with both truth and grace.

What Not to Say

We'll start in this section by looking at the things we shouldn't say or do and then move into how we can support a survivor in a healthy, supportive way.

The section headings below are real statements that were spoken to me, and they're words I've heard echoed by countless survivors. Most came from well-meaning people (family, friends, and church members) who truly believed they were offering comfort or spiritual guidance. But when you've lived through abuse, words like these can deepen wounds instead of healing them. Below, I want to explain why each of these common phrases does more harm than good, and how we can respond in ways that truly help.

"God's timing is perfect. Just trust His plan."

Ouch! While this statement may hold truth in a general sense, it can sound cruel when spoken to someone in the midst of trauma. It implies that abuse is somehow part of God's plan, which twists His character and minimizes the survivor's pain. God's timing *is* perfect, but abuse is never caused or sanctioned by Him. His will is not for us to experience suffering, oppression, or injustice.

Sadly, this phrase has also been used way too often to pressure someone to stay with their abuser. It becomes the doorway to other harmful statements like, "If God wants you to leave, He'll make a way," or, "God hates divorce. If you just pray harder, your husband's heart will change." Words like these re-victimize survivors and heap spiritual guilt on top of their pain.

Instead of trying to mold the sin of abuse into something explainable or tolerable, choose to be supportive. Offer safety, understanding, and the assurance that God's heart is for their safety, not their bondage.

"God won't give you more than you can handle." (1 Corinthians 10:13, NKJV)

"No temptation has overtaken you except what is common to mankind. And God is faithful; he will not let you be tempted beyond what you can bear. But when you are tempted, he will also provide a way out so that you can endure it." 1 Corinthians 10:13 (NKJV)

This verse is often misused and taken out of context. Paul was speaking about temptation, not trauma. Abuse is not a test from God; it's evil inflicted by human choice. When someone is trapped in an abusive situation, they already have *more* than they can handle.

Telling a survivor to endure what's unbearable suggests that God expects them to carry the weight of someone else's sin. That's not truth. God never asks His children to remain in harm's way to prove their faith or strength.

"Have you tried marriage counseling?"

This question assumes the issue is a mutual relationship problem rather than an abuse issue. Marriage counseling is designed for couples who share mutual responsibility in the problem and a desire to repair the issue. Marriage counseling is not for situations where one person is harming, manipulating, or controlling the other.

In fact, joint counseling in abusive relationships is dangerous. It gives the abuser more tools to twist the survivor's words and maintain control. Asking a survivor to attend counseling with their abuser can further endanger them. Someone experiencing abuse doesn't have the freedom to share what the truth is about their situation in a counseling setting. And an abuser is never going to share the truth of their behavior with a therapist.

"Why don't you both come over to our home, and we can talk about it."

I want to be very clear about this, you should **never** put yourself in the role of a mental health professional. Never, never, never. Full stop. You don't have the training, and when you personally know the couple, you also have a bias. It's human nature. You don't want to believe that abuse could happen in your friends' home. You want to believe that healing is possible, if they could only talk through it.

Inviting both people into the same space may seem like a neutral or peacemaking approach, but it's not safe. It assumes both sides are equally valid and that the issue is a simple conflict that can be solved through conversation. It's not. Survivors are rarely able to speak freely in front of their abuser, and doing so can put them in greater danger.

You are not powerful enough to override the conscious choice of someone who is determined to abuse. Abuse is not a misunderstanding, it's a deliberate misuse of power and control. The most loving thing you can do is recognize your limits and help the survivor find individual support through trained professionals while offering your steady, judgment-free presence.

"Everything happens for a reason."

This phrase often becomes a spiritual shortcut, a way to avoid the discomfort of sitting with someone's pain. While it's true that God can redeem even the darkest situations, that doesn't mean He *caused* them. Abuse is never part of His design or will.

I know this may ruffle some feathers, but not everything happens for a reason. God does not cause sin. He doesn't cause trauma or suffering. He promises to be with us through it. He is the One who bends down to lift us when we've been crushed, who gathers the broken pieces and begins to restore what was shattered. He takes His children by the hand and walks with them, one step at a time, on the long road toward healing.

"Forgiving will help you to heal."

Even though I heard this statement from a well-meaning church member, just writing it down makes my stomach turn. Forgiveness is deeply personal and sacred. Pushing someone to forgive while they are still experiencing trauma, or before they are ready, can cause lasting harm. When forgiveness is pressured, it often becomes a tool for silencing pain rather than releasing it to the One who heals. Survivors must first be safe before they can begin to process the spiritual and emotional steps that lead to genuine forgiveness.

Jesus tells us in Luke 17:3-4 (NKJV), "If your brother or sister sins against you, rebuke them; and if they repent, forgive them. Even if they sin against you seven times in a day and seven times come back to you saying 'I repent,' you must forgive them." This passage shows that forgiveness is tied to genuine repentance. But what does "repent" really mean? True repentance involves a heartfelt change and turning away from harmful behavior. If the abusive behavior repeatedly continues despite claims of apology, this is not true repentance. Healing and stepping away from bitterness are not the same as forgiveness, and forgiveness cannot be demanded or rushed.

"I can't imagine him ever being abusive."

Abusers are often skilled at creating a charming, religious, or respectable public image. Doubting a survivor's story because the abuser "doesn't seem like that kind of person" only isolates them further and reinforces the abuser's control.

Have you ever personally witnessed someone being physically or emotionally abused in your church, at work, or even while out shopping? Probably not. That's because abuse is a choice, and it happens intentionally behind closed doors. It is carefully concealed, hidden beneath a veneer of charm, success, or piety. Survivors often fear speaking out because of shame, threats, or concern that no one will believe them.

Abuse thrives in secrecy, and that secrecy is reinforced by society's assumptions about what an "abuser" looks like. An abuser is often portrayed in movies as someone that has visible, frequent anger issues. Someone that constantly scowls, barely speaks when spoken to, and gets in frequent physical altercations. People are conditioned to believe that someone with a good reputation, a church leadership role, or a polished public persona couldn't possibly be capable of causing harm to their spouse or children. This makes it so easy for people to dismiss the lived reality of survivors that contributes to their isolation.

You don't need to understand the full picture, or even part of it, to recognize that abuse is real. Its invisibility doesn't make it less devastating, and its hidden nature doesn't excuse the harm. Acknowledging this truth is an important step in seeing the survivor's experience for what it really is.

"Why did you stay for so long?"

We covered this question at length in the previous chapter, but it's worth repeating it here. One of the most common questions survivors hear is, "Why did you stay for so long?" On the surface, it may seem like a simple question, but for someone who has lived through abuse, it feels like a judgment rather than a genuine way to create open dialogue.

Abuse is not a reflection of a survivor's weakness, moral failure, or lack of faith. It is a pattern of intentional harm inflicted by another person. The decision to stay is often a survival strategy, one that allows the survivor to navigate day-to-day life while protecting themselves as best they can.

The timeline of abuse is rarely linear. Survivors may leave multiple times and return, struggle with conflicting emotions, or spend years planning an escape. Each moment in that journey is shaped by real threats, real fear, and real barriers. Understanding this complexity helps us see that "staying" is not a choice made lightly, but often the only option available in a situation that feels impossible to escape.

What Not to Do

Before we go any further, it's important to state some hard truths. These are not meant to discourage compassion or deter you from helping, but to protect everyone involved. Abuse is complex, dangerous, and almost always hidden. Good intentions alone are not enough to ensure safety.

Setting clear boundaries is essential, not only to protect the survivor, but also to safeguard the people who are trying to help. Overstepping these limits can unintentionally cause more harm, place you in danger, or complicate the survivor's journey to safety and freedom. Understanding what *not* to do creates a foundation of safety, awareness, and wisdom that allows your support to be effective without putting anyone at risk.

Let's look at key actions to avoid, so you can approach this delicate work with care, clarity, and respect for the realities of abuse.

Do not act as a mental health counselor

Even with the best intentions, you are not a trained professional. Mental health counseling requires specialized skills, assessments, and understanding that go far beyond good intentions or personal experience. Attempting to step into this role can unintentionally cause confusion, deepen trauma, or put both you and the survivor at risk. Recognizing your limits is not a failure, it is part of honoring the seriousness of abuse.

Do not try to intervene between the couple

Stepping in to mediate or "fix" a relationship may seem helpful, but it assumes that both parties share equal responsibility or that the situation is a simple conflict. Abuse is never a misunderstanding, it is a deliberate misuse of power and control. Intervening can inadvertently give the abuser more leverage, place the survivor at greater risk, and obscure the reality of the abuse for everyone involved.

Do not try to convince someone to leave or stay

Survivors face complex, layered barriers to leaving an abusive situation, including fear, finances, children, and emotional manipulation. Pressuring them to leave, or stay, reduces the situation to a choice that is far simpler than it actually is. Each survivor's journey is unique, and timing is influenced by real threats, personal safety, and emotional readiness. Attempts to persuade them either way can unintentionally deepen shame, guilt, or fear. It can also cause them to move in a direction that goes against their instincts and put them in greater danger.

Do not turn your home into a shelter

Opening your home may feel like the logical immediate solution, but it can introduce new risks for both you and the survivor. Housing a survivor without proper planning or professional guidance can compromise the survivor's safety, create legal liability, or place your own household in danger. While generosity and compassion are vital, sheltering can transform good intentions into unsafe circumstances.

Do not put yourself in danger

Abuse is a choice made by the abuser, and even the most compassionate person cannot control another's harmful behavior. Attempting to confront or physically intervene can escalate the risk for everyone involved. Recognizing your own limits does not mean you care any less, it is an acknowledgment that safety, for both the survivor and you, must be a priority.

With these important realities laid out, let's explore ways to offer meaningful support to someone who has experienced abuse.

Supporting Someone in Words, Attitude, and Action

Knowing how to support someone who has experienced abuse can feel overwhelming, but it doesn't need to be complicated. The first step is often simply showing up with a listening ear and a compassionate heart. Sometimes, the best words are short, honest, and centered on presence rather than solutions. You might say:

- "I don't know what to say, but I am here to support you."

- "I am so sorry you are experiencing this."

- "How can I help?"

- "What are some challenges that you need help with right now?"

- "What do you need to feel safe?"

- "I am here if you want to talk."

These statements communicate belief, care, and presence. They do not try to fix the situation, rush healing, or get more of the nitty gritty details. They simply honor the survivor's experience and affirm that they are not alone.

Attitude Matters

Be kind and courteous, even when the conversation is difficult

Kindness and courtesy are the foundation of any supportive relationship. Survivors may share experiences that are raw, painful, or difficult to hear. Even when you feel uncomfortable, choosing gentle words, a calm tone, and a patient presence communicates respect and care. Your demeanor signals that you are a safe person to speak with, that they are being heard, and that their pain is valid. Small acts of kindness: listening without interruption, making eye contact, or simply being present, can provide profound comfort.

Remember, you don't need to solve their problems

Simply listening and connecting is powerful. I know it's natural to want to fix things for someone you care about, but trying to solve a survivor's challenges can oftentimes do more harm than good. Simply listening, validating their feelings, and showing you are consistently present is often far more meaningful than offering solutions. Connection itself is powerful. It communicates, "I see you, I believe you, and I will walk alongside you." For someone who has experienced isolation or control, that alone can be life-changing.

Focus on understanding how they feel, not how you might feel in the same circumstances

It's easy to fall into the trap of comparing your own experiences or imagining how you would respond in a similar situation. But each survivor's journey is unique, shaped by fear, manipulation, and circumstance. Instead of projecting your feelings or expectations, strive to truly understand their perspective. Ask questions, listen attentively, and let them share their reality on their terms. Empathy, not judgment or comparison, creates a space for genuine trust.

Remember that someone who has recently escaped abuse most likely cannot take in the weight of your shared experience. There may eventually come a time when it's appropriate for you to share your story with them. If you have experienced abuse and are now walking alongside survivors in their journey, simply saying that you are a survivor too can make all the difference in the world. Pray that God will show you when the time is right to reveal more of your story to a survivor.

Reassure them that they are not alone, and express gratitude that they trusted you enough to share

Survivors often carry shame and secrecy, resulting in a self-imposed isolation following their separation or divorce. Acknowledging their courage in speaking up can be validating and empowering. Reassure them that they are not alone, that they are seen, and that you are thankful for their trust. Simply recognizing the bravery it takes to share their story can strengthen their sense of safety and hope. Gratitude and affirmation communicate that their voice matters and that you are committed to walking alongside them, not judging or abandoning them.

Give yourself grace. Supporting a survivor is emotionally challenging, and it is okay to acknowledge your own limits and need for support

Being a source of support for someone who has experienced abuse can be draining, emotionally heavy, and even overwhelming at times. It's important to acknowledge your own limitations and practice self-care. Giving yourself grace doesn't mean stepping away from care, it means recognizing that you cannot carry this burden alone and that it is okay to seek guidance, support of another advocate, and prayer for yourself. Your well-being matters too and maintaining it allows you to continue showing up consistently for the survivor.

Practical Ways to Support

Actions often speak louder than words and showing up for someone who has experienced abuse is one of the clearest ways to reflect Christ's love in action. Genuine care is not only expressed through what we say, but through the consistency of our presence, the respect we give, and the safe space we help to create. Many survivors have heard promises of love before, only to have those words used against them. That's why our actions matter so deeply, they rebuild trust where trust has been broken. Practical, compassionate support helps survivors experience God's love in real, tangible ways, reminding them that they are seen, valued, and never alone.

For me, this kind of support came through two incredible women in my life. My sister, Ann, surrounded me with prayer, encouragement, Bible verses, and the blessing of her time. She drove across the country to help me move. We talked daily on the phone, sometimes multiple times a day when I felt like I couldn't breathe. Her presence reminded me I was not alone, and that God's love could be reflected through someone's hands and words. My friend, Becky offered a different kind of refuge. She was local so meeting her for dinner was often the only time I could eat more than a few bites, because in her company I could finally relax and let my mind and body decompress. She prayed for me and invited me to attend church with her. If it wasn't for her, I probably would not have stepped foot in church for many years. Neither one of these beautiful women had an agenda that they were pushing; they simply loved and supported me in whatever way I needed. Their example showed me that true support is rooted in presence, patience, and unconditional care.

Pray for their protection, healing, and courage.

Prayer is one of the most powerful ways you can come alongside a survivor. Pray that God will surround them with peace, safety, and strength as they take each step toward healing. Ask Him to guide your own words and actions too, so that you can be a source of comfort rather than pressure. And don't just pray for them, offer to pray with them. Even if you cannot be physically present, prayer keeps you connected through God's presence and power.

Believe their story and validate their experience without judgment.

One of the most healing gifts you can offer is belief. When someone shares their story, especially one involving abuse, they are taking a brave and vulnerable step. Avoid questioning or doubting, instead, affirming their courage and acknowledging the pain they have endured. Validation helps restore dignity and begins to rebuild the trust that abuse destroys.

Listen actively, offering your full attention and presence.

Active listening means setting aside distractions and focusing fully on what the survivor is saying, not just their words, but their emotions. Resist the urge to interrupt or offer quick fixes. Sometimes, silence and attentive presence speak more deeply than advice. When someone feels heard and understood, it becomes easier for them to believe that healing is possible.

Stay in touch, providing consistent, dependable connection over time.

Healing doesn't happen overnight. Regular check-ins (a text, a call, or a coffee invitation) remind the survivor that they are not forgotten.

Consistency helps rebuild trust and stability, which are often shattered by abuse. Even small gestures of care communicate that they are valued and that their life matters.

Help them remain connected to the church or community.

Offering a supportive network that values safety and well-being is invaluable. Isolation is one of the abuser's strongest tools. Helping survivors maintain (or potentially rebuild) safe, healthy connections within their faith community may be the only lifeline someone has. Encourage participation in church life without pushing or forcing involvement. Offer practical help, like transportation or introductions to people in the church that volunteer on the abuse prevention team. A loving community is a powerful reminder that God's family is a place of refuge, not judgment.

The presence of people like Ann and Becky shows how these actions look in real life. Their support was consistent, judgment-free, and attuned to my needs rather than their own. That kind steady, patient, and humble love, shows a survivor the reflection of Christ's heart in human form.

****

Supporting someone who has experienced abuse is both challenging and delicate work. It requires patience, humility, and a willingness to walk alongside them without judgment or agenda. While the road may be difficult, your presence, belief, and consistent care can make a profound difference in a survivor's journey toward safety and healing. Remember, your role is not to fix, rescue, or control the situation; it is to offer steady support, prayer, and connection.

Understanding what to say, what not to say, and how to show up with both compassion and wisdom lays the foundation for truly helping without causing harm.

A Prayer for Those Who Support Survivors

Heavenly Father,

Thank You for entrusting us with the incredible responsibility of walking beside those who are hurting. Give us hearts that listen before they speak, and the wisdom to know when to be still and when to act. Help us to reflect Your gentleness and love in every word and gesture, offering comfort without control, and presence without pressure.

Lord, strengthen our spirits when the weight of another's pain feels heavy. Remind us that we are not the healer, You are. Teach us to surrender everything into Your capable hands. Fill us with compassion that does not grow weary and faith that believes You are working even when we cannot see it.

Protect our hearts from fear, discouragement, and burnout. Surround us with Your peace so that we can be steady and safe for others. And as we offer support, remind us to care for our own souls, returning again and again to Your presence for communion with You.

May every act of kindness, every whispered prayer, and every tear shed become an offering of love that honors You and brings hope to those who have suffered.

In Jesus' name, Amen.

Chapter Gate Reminder:
The following chapter continues anonymized, paraphrased recollections intended to protect privacy.

Chapter 11: A Brave New Chapter

I am so excited to share with you that my life looks so vastly different now. When I began preparing to escape, my tears wouldn't stop falling. My mind was clouded in trauma fog, and I could barely form a coherent sentence. Sleep was impossible, I was constantly worried about my children's safety. I lost 30 pounds in 30 days because my stomach was constantly churning, and even a few bites of food would make me sick. Each night, as I laid my head on the pillow, I wondered how I would make ends meet, how I could keep my job when my brain seemed stuck in neutral. I was afraid of my own shadow.

Now, all these years later, I am remarried and sitting on my couch writing a book about abuse recovery and God's unfailing love. My little orange tabby, Mango, is curled up and purring beside me, and candles flicker softly on the coffee table. In the next room, I can hear my amazingly supportive husband talking on the phone to my daughter's fiancé. Both of my children are successfully launched, living their best lives, and strongly supportive of this beautiful ministry to help those that are hurting. My daughter and I have even had the pleasure of giving an abuse prevention seminar together. I have been blessed with two stepdaughters who are beautiful inside and out, and they've brought a new kind of joy and fullness to my heart. Blending our families didn't happen in an absolutely seamless and perfect way, but it's been filled with love and so much grace.

In my world today there are no eggshells to tiptoe around in our home. I know I can stand on my own two feet, but I also know that my biggest cheerleader is the man I am honored to call my husband. I'm surrounded by love and a strong support system in our children, my sister, mother-in-law and father-in-law, my sister-in-law, and so many beautiful women I am honored to call my friends. And these days, when my head touches the pillow, I fall asleep with peace instead of fear.

Life looks so beautifully different now.

Reflecting on the Journey

There were so many moments when I never thought I'd make it through. Healing didn't happen overnight. It came in quiet steps, through tears in a counselor's office, drives to work where I talked to God out loud, and in moments when I questioned everything I thought I knew about myself. Some days I felt strong, ready to stand up for everything I believed in. Other days, I barely had the strength to get out of bed, forcing myself to keep going for my kids and as an example to them. But with time, and a lot of grace, the fog began to lift.

It took a long time, but I finally started to recognize my own voice again. I learned to trust my instincts instead of silencing them. I realized that courage isn't always loud or flashy, sometimes it's simply showing up for the next day.

I remember so clearly when a friend called, trying to push me into living my life the way she thought I should. She had set timelines and milestones for my life that she wanted me to follow. I set a boundary, gently letting her know she wasn't in control of my life, my choices, or my journey moving forward. Her response was, "You're not the same sweet Michelle I used to know." I stayed silent, thinking to myself, *"You only thought I was sweet before because I never had the courage to maintain the boundaries I set."* When I stayed silent, she said a quick goodbye and hung up, and over time, our calls became fewer and fewer. And that is ok.

Moments like that phone call taught me something powerful: standing up for myself often meant standing alone, at least at first. But each boundary I set, each small act of courage, became a stepping stone toward freedom. Over time, I began to notice how different life felt when I wasn't bending to everyone else's expectations. I started to experience the quiet joys I'd thought were gone forever, the comfort of a home where I could breathe, the peace of sleep that didn't come with knots in my stomach, and the ability to trust myself again. These were the first glimpses of my new normal, the life I was learning to claim as my own.

My new normal doesn't mean life is perfect. Old fears still whisper sometimes, and I still have moments when the past creeps in unexpectedly. Many of the wounds have healed, but there are still scars that can be seen when you look close enough. But now I have tools to meet those moments with courage in the face of fear. There are still times when I smell something or hear something that takes me back to a time in my life where fear ruled the day. I've learned to pause, breathe, and ask God for wisdom and strength to handle those moments. I've learned that boundaries aren't walls to shut people out, they are gates that protect the growth and healing inside me.

Faith became my anchor through it all. I began to understand that God's love didn't leave me in the darkness; it carried me through it. Even in the hardest seasons, He placed people in my life, provided unexpected blessings, and whispered hope in quiet, unexpected ways. One verse that carried me through those early years was Isaiah 43:2 (NKJV): *"When you pass through the waters, I will be with you; and through the rivers, they shall not overflow you."* That promise is such a beautiful encouragement to me, reminding me that even in the deepest waters, I am never alone.

There were times when I needed to be reminded of that truth in tangible ways, moments when I was desperate to know that God still saw me. One day, in the midst of my abusive marriage, I sat alone in my back yard, weighed down by fear and discouragement. Through tears, I whispered a simple prayer: *"Lord, please show me that You still see me. That You still care."* As I sat there, a dragonfly landed gently on my knee. It startled me at first, but then I felt this quiet peace wash over me. It was as if God was saying, *"I'm still here. I haven't left you."*

A short time later, on my birthday, I was sitting at my desk at work. My heart was heavy with the reality of my failing marriage and the raw, painful process of divorce. I quietly prayed again, asking God to remind me that He still loved me. A coworker suddenly called out, "Look out the window!" When I turned my head, I was stunned to see thousands of dragonflies rising from the grassy yard outside our office. Their wings shimmering in the sunlight. I couldn't hold back the tears. From that day until my divorce was finalized, nearly six months later, I saw a dragonfly every single day. It became my personal reminder that I was not forgotten. When I shared with a friend that the dragonfly wasn't coming any longer, she showed up with a brass dragonfly paperweight to put on my desk, a constant reminder that God is always with me.

Years later, when I was dating my now husband, I shared the story of the dragonflies with him and our children. We were standing in a lake on a warm afternoon, laughing together. I told them how I believed that God sent dragonflies to remind me of His faithfulness. As I spoke, a dragonfly landed on my husband's shoulder. My eyes filled with tears as I felt that same gentle whisper from God: *"See? I'm still with you."*

When we had our wedding, our daughters each wore a small dragonfly charm in their hair, and I carried that same charm in my bridal bouquet. It was my quiet reminder of God's faithfulness through every chapter of my life, from despair to healing, from fear to freedom.

To this day, whenever I see a dragonfly, I smile. It's what I call a "God wink," a reminder that even when life feels uncertain, He is near, watching over me, guiding me, and writing beauty into every new beginning.

God didn't remove every storm from my life, but He taught me to look for His presence within them. Each dragonfly became a small symbol of hope, a whisper that beauty can rise even from broken places. Over time, I realized that I just needed to be still and know (Psalm 46:10, NKJV). Sometimes that meant being still long enough to notice the ways God was showing me that I wasn't alone, He is always with me.

In those still moments, something began to change within me. The same God who met me in my brokenness was now teaching me how to live with strength and purpose. Healing wasn't about forgetting what I'd been through but about learning how to help others because of it.

With every passing day, courage began to look different to me. It wasn't about proving myself to anyone else. It wasn't loud or flashy. Courage, to me, meant that I was choosing to get out of bed, choosing to trust myself, choosing to let God guide me one step at a time. And as courage grew, so did the ability to dream again. I started to imagine possibilities I had long buried, the hope of a life filled with peace, love, and purpose. Writing this book is one of those dreams. So is walking alongside women who are navigating the same hard path I once walked.

Healing doesn't erase the past, it redeems it. It allows you to look back and say, *"That chapter hurt, but it wasn't the end of my story."* Every small victory, every moment of joy, every breath of peace is proof that the next chapter can be brave, even if the pages are still being written.

My friend, you have the ability to pick up the pen and write your next brave chapter. That blank page is waiting for you whenever you're ready. I know that when you are still processing grief, working through the mess, and trying to figure out the next right step, it can feel impossible to imagine your life looking any different than it does right now. But I'm here to encourage you today to keep dreaming, keep striving, keep moving toward the goals God has placed in your heart.

Having courage doesn't mean you are not afraid. It means choosing to move forward even when fear is standing in your way. It means saying, *"I will take the next step, even if I can't see the whole path."*

I promise you, God has you in His hand. He sees your fears, your needs, and the desires of your heart. He knows the weight you carry, the doubts that creep in during those quiet moments, and the prayers you may feel too afraid to speak aloud. He is faithful to guide you, step by step, into the life He has planned for you.

Practical Ways to Begin Your Next Brave Chapter

1. Start Small

You don't have to rewrite your whole life at once. Begin with one small step, something that reminds you that you have control over your choices. It might be setting a boundary, saying "no" to something that drains you, or taking a few minutes each day to do something that brings you joy. Maybe it's sitting on your porch and enjoying a quiet cup of tea in the morning sunlight, or carving out a few minutes for prayer, journaling, or a nature walk. Small victories build confidence and momentum. Each little step is proof that you are reclaiming your life and your power, one choice at a time.

2. Reflect and Reimagine

Take some quiet time to reflect on where you've been and where you want to go. Journaling can be a powerful tool here. Write down your dreams, your hopes, and even your fears. Then, think about what your life could look like if fear didn't hold you back. Picture it in detail: the people, the places, the feelings. What does safety feel like? What does joy look like in your home? Let yourself believe that a new chapter is possible, even if it feels distant right now. Reflection is the first step toward reclaiming your dreams for the future.

3. Surround Yourself with Support

You don't have to walk this journey alone. Seek out people who will encourage you, pray for you, and celebrate even the smallest steps forward. Sometimes support comes from friends, family, or mentors. Sometimes it comes from connecting (or reconnecting) with your faith community or professional counselors and coaches. Wherever it comes from, make the time and space for it. Sharing your journey doesn't make you weak, it makes you human, and having support helps you stay grounded and accountable as you take brave steps forward.

4. Lean on Faith

Keep God at the center of your next chapter. Pray over your dreams, your decisions, and even your fears. Trust that He is guiding your steps and that He has a plan for you that is better than any dream you could imagine. Scripture can be a lifeline when doubt or fear creeps in. Verses like Jeremiah 29:11 remind us that He has plans to give us hope and a future. Lean into your faith not just in the big moments, but in the everyday moments too. Even small prayers, whispered in quiet moments, can give clarity, courage, and peace that carry you forward.

5. Celebrate Courage, Not Just Success

Courage isn't measured by perfection or how quickly things change for the better. It's measured by your willingness to keep moving forward despite your fears. Celebrate the small acts of bravery, the times you stand in truth, set a boundary, ask for help, or speak up for yourself. These are the moments that lead to real transformation. Every brave choice, no matter how small, is proof that your story is unfolding and that healing is within reach.

My friend, each day you take even one intentional step toward your dreams, you are rewriting your story. God has been walking with you in every chapter, He will not leave you now. Your next brave chapter is waiting, and it begins whenever you are ready to pick up the pen and start writing.

Your story is still being written, and the next chapter is yours to shape. You may feel uncertain, afraid, or still in a tangled mess that feels overwhelming. But that doesn't mean you aren't brave. Bravery is not the absence of fear; it is moving forward even when fear is present.

Please take a moment to breathe and reflect on how far you've come. Every step you've taken, every boundary you've set, every tear you've cried, it has all brought you to this place of possibility. The possibility of living a life untangled from abuse. Healing doesn't erase the past, but it equips you to step into the future with hope, faith, and courage.

Remember, God holds your story in His hands. He sees your heart, He knows your fears, and He delights in your dreams. Your next chapter doesn't need to be perfect, it just needs to be intentionally written, one courageous step at a time.

I believe in you and I'm praying for you.

Trust Him. Keep moving forward. Your brave new chapter is waiting, and it is filled with hope, restoration, and life beyond what you imagined possible.

Closing Prayer

Heavenly Father,

Thank You for walking with us through every dark valley, every moment of fear, and every tear we've cried. Thank You for holding us when we felt we couldn't stand, and for guiding our steps when the path seemed unclear.

Lord, I lift up every reader of this book to You. I ask that You fill their hearts with courage when fear tries to hold them back, with hope when the weight of the past feels heavy, and with peace in the knowledge that You are always near. Help them to see themselves as You see them, worthy, beloved, and capable of living untangled from a life of abuse.

Grant them the wisdom to set healthy boundaries, the strength to rise after setbacks, and the faith to trust Your timing in every part of their journey. Let them celebrate even the smallest victories, knowing that each step forward is a step toward a beautiful new life in You.

Lord, may every broken piece of their story be redeemed, every wound healed in Your perfect love, and every dream restored according to Your plan. Help them to pick up the pen of their life with confidence, trusting that You are already writing the next chapter alongside them.

In Jesus' name, Amen.

Resources
Please contact 911 if you feel that you are in a life-threatening or dangerous situation.

Resources for Support and Healing in the United States

If you or someone you know is experiencing domestic abuse, the following organizations offer confidential, compassionate assistance:

National Domestic Violence Hotline
- **Phone**: 1-800-799-SAFE (7233)
- **Text**: START to 88788
- **Website**: thehotline.org
- Available 24/7, providing support in over 200 languages.

National Coalition Against Domestic Violence (NCADV)
- **Website**: ncadv.org
- Advocates for policy change and provides resources for survivors.

National Network to End Domestic Violence (NNEDV)
- **Website**: nnedv.org
- Supports state coalitions and offers resources for survivors and advocates.

National Resource Center on Domestic Violence (NRCDV)
- **Website**: nrcdv.org
- Provides training, technical assistance, and resources for advocates and survivors.

WomensLaw.org
- **Website**: womenslaw.org
- Offers legal information and resources for survivors of domestic violence.

StrongHearts Native Helpline
- **Phone/Text**: 1-844-762-8483
- **Website**: strongheartshelpline.org
- A confidential, culturally appropriate helpline for Native Americans affected by domestic violence.

About the Author

Michelle Perez is a speaker and writer with a passion for helping others find healing, hope, and purpose after brokenness. As a survivor of domestic abuse, she has dedicated her voice to raising awareness, equipping others to recognize the signs of unhealthy relationships, and guiding organizations to  become safer spaces for those in crisis. Through her seminars, Michelle teaches on topics such as emotional intelligence, conflict resolution, and identifying red flags in relationships, all anchored in biblical truth and grace.

In addition to her work in abuse prevention, Michelle is deeply committed to empowering Christian women in leadership and supporting blended families as they navigate faith, love, and restoration. Her heart for ministry reflects her belief that God can redeem every story and use it for His glory.

Michelle holds a bachelor's degree in business management and a master's degree in management and leadership. She lives in Pennsylvania, where her husband serves as a pastor.

Her upcoming books, *Leading Untangled* and *Loving Untangled*, will continue her mission to help others lead and love with wholeness and wisdom after seasons of hardship. Michelle regularly speaks at churches, conferences, and women's events, inspiring audiences to embrace God's truth, reclaim their hope, and walk in freedom.

Website: www.UntangledJourney.com

www.ingramcontent.com/pod-product-compliance
Lightning Source LLC
Chambersburg PA
CBHW071631140626
46555CB00022B/2255